T0318796

Cambridge Elements ≡

Elements in Public Policy
edited by
M. Ramesh
National University of Singapore (NUS)
Michael Howlett
Simon Fraser University, British Columbia
Xun WU
Hong Kong University of Science and Technology
Judith Clifton
University of Cantabria
Eduardo Araral
National University of Singapore (NUS)

PUBLIC INQUIRIES AND POLICY DESIGN

Alastair Stark
University of Queensland

Sophie Yates
Australian National University

CAMBRIDGE
UNIVERSITY PRESS

Shaftesbury Road, Cambridge CB2 8EA, United Kingdom

One Liberty Plaza, 20th Floor, New York, NY 10006, USA

477 Williamstown Road, Port Melbourne, VIC 3207, Australia

314–321, 3rd Floor, Plot 3, Splendor Forum, Jasola District Centre, New Delhi – 110025, India

103 Penang Road, #05–06/07, Visioncrest Commercial, Singapore 238467

Cambridge University Press is part of Cambridge University Press & Assessment, a department of the University of Cambridge.

We share the University's mission to contribute to society through the pursuit of education, learning and research at the highest international levels of excellence.

www.cambridge.org
Information on this title: www.cambridge.org/9781009494489

DOI: 10.1017/9781009286879

First published 2024

A catalogue record for this publication is available from the British Library.

ISBN 978-1-009-49448-9 Hardback
ISBN 978-1-009-28689-3 Paperback
ISSN 2398-4058 (online)
ISSN 2514-3565 (print)

Public Inquiries and Policy Design

Elements in Public Policy

DOI: 10.1017/9781009286879
First published online: January 2024

Alastair Stark
University of Queensland

Sophie Yates
Australian National University

Author for correspondence: Alastair Stark, alastair.stark@uq.edu.au

Abstract: Public inquiries regularly produce outcomes of importance to policy design. However, the policy design literature has largely ignored the many important ways that public inquiries can act as policy design tools, meaning the functions that inquiries can offer the policy designer are not properly understood. This Element addresses this gap in two ways. First, it presents a theoretical discussion, underpinned by international empirical illustrations, to explain how inquiries perform policy design roles and can be classified as procedural policy tools. It focuses on four inquiry functions – catalytic, learning, processual, and legitimation. Second, it addresses the challenge of designing inquiries that have the policy-facing capacities required to make them effective. It introduces plurality as a key variable influencing effectiveness, demonstrating its relevance to internal inquiry operations, the external inquiry environment, and policy tool selection. Thus, it combines conceptual and practical insights to speak to academic and practice orientated audiences.

Keywords: public inquiries, policy design, policy learning, policy tools, implementation

ISBNs: 9781009494489 (HB), 9781009286893 (PB), 9781009286879 (OC)
ISSNs: 2398-4058 (online), 2514-3565 (print)

Contents

1 The Public Inquiry: An Idiosyncratic Institution

Public inquiries are highly idiosyncratic organisations that exist outside the rhythm of everyday politics and policymaking. Their independence from government means that they need not operate in a typical bureaucratic manner when going about their work. The politics of organisational survival does not concern them as they are well funded and purposefully created to have a short shelf life. They exist primarily to communicate policy advice but not to action it, which means they are free from the burden of implementation and service delivery. And they tend to be staffed by professionals who have been successful in their 'day jobs' and therefore expect to be given autonomy and agency to make decisions on their own terms. These characteristics all mean that inquiries have the capacity to do things differently. As a consequence, we see a great of deal of variance in inquiries around the world, both in their form and functioning, and in the menu of political, social and policy-orientated outputs that they deliver.

Scholars interested in public inquiries reflect the variance that can be found in their unit of analysis, which means that the literature on these institutions is both voluminous and inter-disciplinary. Unsurprisingly, researchers tend to bring their discipline's characteristics into their studies. Sociologists, for example, 'abstract up' to reflect on the role that inquiries play in relation to larger structural forces (Ashforth 1990) or they use textual analyses to 'dig down' into inquiry texts in order to see those larger structures staring back at them (Brown 2000). Law scholars also focus on what we might expect from their discipline, by either examining procedural processes at the organisational level from a practitioner perspective (Beer 2011; Mitchell et al. 2020) or exploring larger notions of justice and representation in a more scholarly manner (Schwartz 1997; Salter 2007). Some political scientists have delivered rather pessimistic evaluations of the public inquiry that suggest they are a manifestation of executive (and therefore elite) power and largely ineffectual as a consequence (Clokie and Robinson 1937; Bulmer 1980; Sulitzeanu-Kenan 2010). However, political science and policy studies have also produced the largest and most consistent body of inquiry literature. In this field, we can find a series of contemporary works from policy facing political scientists who have developed frameworks, taxonomies and detailed analyses to illustrate the policy relevance and important contributions of public inquiries (see, e.g., Inwood and Johns 2014; Marier 2017; Stark 2019; Stanton 2022; Prasser 2023). Some have also extended the analysis of inquiries through the systematic generation of data about their role within specific political cultures (e.g., Christensen and Holst 2017; Hesstvedt and Christiansen 2022; Hesstvedt and Christensen 2023).

The fact that these political scientists have made consistent contributions to the study of inquiries over time, and developed frameworks for studying and classifying them, means that the scholarship in this area has become more coherent over the past decade. However, what distinguishes inquiry literature from other branches of political science is the massive constellation of one-off studies that have made claims about these institutions. These studies mean that, like inquiries themselves, the literature is very idiosyncratic. Scholars from a large variety of disciplines have tended to stumble across an inquiry that has piqued their interest, usually because the inquiry has conducted work on their specific research area. These particular inquiries are analysed, their work and importance are speculated upon and then after a single publication they are typically abandoned as a research concern. This has implications both for the quality of knowledge that we have about inquiries and for the coherence of this body of literature (see Stark 2019) because the morass of single shot studies surrounds the core body of work noted above with varying forms of commentary. This variation means that we need to be very clear about the particular focus and contribution of this Element.

To clarify our contribution, we first offer a definition of what we mean when we use the term public inquiry and then discuss the variety of functions that inquiries can perform in greater detail. When it comes to definition, we use the term public inquiry simply to denote those institutions that represent 'temporary working groups created, mandated and made independent by governments in order to fact-find, hold actors to account or develop policy lessons' (Stark and Yates 2021: 347). This is an expansive definition that allows us to discuss 'blue-ribbon' commissions of inquiry and large-scale inquiries constituted through legislation alongside less formal policy reviews and expert-driven advisory commissions such as task forces. While each sub-type has its own defining characteristics – for example, task forces tend to be set up on a smaller scale, with more explicit design mandates and fewer formal investigative powers (Inwood and Johns 2022) – they have some similarities that allow us to consider them together. Therefore, we set boundaries on what is in and out of the analysis with specific reference to five defining characteristics, which we argue represent the essence of the public inquiry. These tell us that public inquiries are: 1) independent, to varying degrees, from executive control or state influence; 2) open to public involvement in terms of the generation of evidence; 3) responsible for the delivery (but not implementation) of policy advice; 4) highly contingent in terms of form and function; and 5) temporary in terms of existence (see Stark and Yates 2021: 347–8 for a fuller discussion of each of these characteristics).

We can also think about inquiries as the producers of four categories of output. It is certainly the case that inquiries are convened to produce *political outputs*. The announcement of a public inquiry, for example, often offers the chance to release political pressure or to cool an issue down by removing it temporarily from an intense political spotlight (Herbert 1961; Elliot and McGuiness 2002; Stark et al. 2023). Alternatively, it has been said that inquiries can be steered from a distance in a way that ensures that their recommendations favour the interests of those who have convened it (Bulmer 1980; Ashforth 1990). A great deal of attention has been given to these agenda management functions in the public inquiry literature (Sulitzeanu-Kenan 2010; Marier 2017). Most of it paints a rather depressing picture of the inquiry either as an enfeebled institution that can be easily outmanoeuvred by elites who wish to ignore its recommendations or – worse still – as a marionette that can be made to dance to the tune of an executive master. Such caricatures have been criticised for underplaying the complexity of contemporary policymaking and the nature of twenty-first century politics (Stark 2020), yet their allure remains compelling to some commentators who continue to define inquiries as agenda management mechanisms (e.g., McConnell 2020: 964).

However, if we shift the lens upwards and away from the dark arts of politics, it is clear that inquiries can play a reparative role within political systems. When failings damage legitimacy, support and stability within a polity, the convening of a mechanism that has the potential to account and remedy issues becomes important (Boin et al. 2016: 115–7). These systemic political outcomes materialise because inquiries can produce *social-psychological outputs* that have profoundly symbolic effects. When inquiries allow victims to tell their stories and feel represented, when they deliver diagnoses that explain uncertainty and, above all, when they present the appearance (whether real or artificial) of action and change, inquiries produce these outputs (Renå and Christensen 2020). However, inquiry scholars debate the value of these symbolic outputs and many who write from a power-critical perspective tend to argue that they are problematic. These criticisms suggest that inquiries can produce political outputs that re-legitimate problematic status quos, award certain voices status while ignoring others, and offer up conclusions that help executives avoid radical reform (Ashforth 1990; Brown 2004; Vaughan 2006; Boudes and Laroche 2009).

Legal scholars have also given a great deal of attention to public inquiries, which reflects the outputs that they can produce in relation to *administrative justice*. In this regard, inquiries have been described as part of the 'fourth branch of government' (Donson and O'Donovan 2022: 138) because of their capacity to produce oversight and accountability in relation to political, bureaucratic and judicial decision-making. At one end of a process, inquiries can represent 'a final accountability backstop' (Donson and O'Donovan 2022: 138) when other avenues of accountability have failed. At the start of another process, the evidence produced by inquiries can be passed to prosecutors who may wish to begin proceedings if it shows negligence, maladministration or criminality. However, beyond these specific legal outputs, law scholars have also shown how inquiries produce forms of representation and restorative justice through truth telling and hindsight reconstruction (McAlinden and Naylor 2016; Stanton 2022) and forms of public deliberation that shape policy debates (Donson and O'Donovan 2022: 142). The importance of these legal outputs, combined with the fact that many inquiries are staffed by legal personnel, has also led legal scholars to produce research which is orientated towards the practitioner (Beer 2011) ranging from the very procedural and pragmatic (Mitchell et al. 2020) to the more theoretical end of constitutional law (Ratushny 2009).

Finally, and most importantly, public inquiries produce outputs of relevance to the delivery of *public policy*. Less research exists in this area. However, policy researchers have already established that inquiries can perform 'policy learning' functions (Stark 2018) and that their institutional features can offer the impetus for policy change more broadly (Inwood and Johns 2014; Resodihardjo 2020; Mintrom et al. 2021). Quite simply, policy scholars understand that these institutions can have transformative policy effects. Indeed, Johns and Inwood (2018) note that in Canada, it is difficult to think of a policy area that has *not* been influenced by a public inquiry. However, even if an inquiry's recommendations are not substantively implemented, its work can still influence policy indirectly by shaping public debate, providing an ideational touchstone and a reference point for activists, and influencing the way policy is evaluated in a particular domain (Althaus 1994; Cunneen 2001; Stark 2018). The purpose of this Element is to contribute to this strand of inquiry scholarship so that we can better understand the variety of policy roles inquiries perform.

More specifically, we are concerned with the ways in which public inquiries can produce *policy design outputs*. We therefore view inquiries in this Element as *policy design tools,* which can equip those who must formulate policy with the means to perform a range of roles. Even more specifically, to use the parlance of policy design, we view public inquiries as procedural policy tools (Stark and Yates 2021), as they do not deliver policy directly but significantly influence the rules of the game around it (see Howlett 2000).

The decision to study inquiries as policy tools means that this Element is primarily seeking to locate and study the public inquiry within that sub-field of policy studies that relates to policy design and formulation (for a comprehensive overview, see Howlett and Mukherjee 2017). Ultimately therefore, this is an

Element about public inquiries for policy scholars. However, it is also an Element about policy design for public inquiry scholars. In relation to each community, the task remains the same: to deliver an analysis of the ways in which public inquiries can act as policy design tools. Our contribution is primarily conceptual but it is also practical. We set out concepts that connect policy design and public inquiry together (see Section 2), we draw on empirical examples, and illuminate our arguments with evidence from a range of international contexts, but our intention is to speak to the real-world challenges associated with producing outcomes through policy design and public inquiry processes. We aim to show that policy designers – by which we mean 'people working in and around government whose primary role is to craft proposals for policy directions' (Mintrom and Luetjens 2017: 176) – have much in common with inquiry members and supporting staff. In the process, we explicate four main policy design roles or functions of public inquiries: catalytic, learning, processual and legitimation (Section 3). We are also concerned with inquiry effectiveness, both in general and with respect to their policy design functions (Section 4). This means we are concerned in this Element both with *the policy design roles of public inquiries* and *the design of inquiries for policy design purposes*. Having established this, the most obvious question to turn to next is: what exactly is policy design? Addressing this question also helps us to refine our focus.

2 Theorising Inquiries as Policy Tools

2.1 The Focus on Policy Design

We can initially cut through the dizzying array of taxonomies, types and classifications that exist in the sub-field of policy design in order to say something rather simple, which is that policy design scholarship can be understood in terms of three questions. First, to simplify in the extreme: what is the thinking behind a policy's core assumptions? Here, the challenge is to understand the way in which intellectual schemas, typically reflected in ideal-type cause-and-effect claims, shape the fundamental thinking behind policy options and configurations (see Linders and Peters 1988 and Peters et al. 2018). Second, what instruments can act as means to the desired policy end? In this area, research has expended a great deal of time and energy defining the nature and effects of specific policy tools, and combinations of tools, that are built or chosen by policy designers (see Jordan and Turnpenny 2015). Finally, how is policy formulated? Addressing this question means understanding the processes and procedures through which policy advice is generated, delivered and schemes and tools selected (see Howlett 2009).

This may sound like a crude attempt to simplify a complex field with many moving parts, but what is important here is that in all three of these efforts, policy scholars try hard to produce practice-orientated knowledge. This is what distinguishes policy design research from other branches of the policy sciences in which the gap between theory and practice is much wider. One of the reasons for this narrowed gap is that policy design scholarship accepts, to different degrees depending on the author and the work, that design thinking is ultimately about effective and efficient goal attainment, which requires 'processes of more or less conscious and *rational* efforts at design' (Howlett 2011: 22, emphasis added). Introducing the r word into any policy writing in the twenty-first century can be a fraught endeavour but there is no escaping the fact that policy design scholarship commits to what Stone (2012) once defined as the 'rationality project'. To be clear, no one knows the irrationality, uncertainty and sheer contingency that characterise the social world more than the policy designer and the policy design scholar. Both are doomed to analyse repeated failures, precisely because of the many and varied ways that policy and its objects are 'irrational'. As Peters et al. (2018: 32) note, policy design is purposive and instrumental but it must also understand feasibility and acceptance (and their opposites). What is crucial to understand, however, is that despite being well recognised and well understood (see, e.g., Howlett 2019, 2020), these factors have not stopped a continued effort to better execute design functions. For the purposes of this Element, this means accepting that the analysis of inquiries must be calibrated towards evaluating the extent to which they can offer *utility* to the policy designer. This takes us directly to the following well-known definition of policy design as:

> "the effort to more or less systematically develop efficient and effective policies through *the application of knowledge about policy means gained from experience, and reason, to the development and adoption of courses of action* that are likely to succeed in attaining their desired goals or aims within specific policy contexts" (Howlett 2011: 22, emphasis added).

In relation to our intention to study the inquiry as a policy design tool, this definition, and its encapsulation of the practice-orientated focus of design studies, is helpful because it moves us towards a selective study of the public inquiry. It does this by encouraging us to give attention to the inquiry functions (and research) which have specific utility to the policy designer and to do so at the expense of other aspects of the public inquiry, which are certainly important, but not necessarily applicable to instrumental design thinking. These omissions encompass the research that explores the political 'agenda management' functions discussed above (e.g., Acland 1980; Ashforth 1990; Prasser 1994, Stark 2020), and that which documents the ways in which inquiries produce problematic social-psychological outputs (e.g., Gephart 1993; Brown 2004; Vaughan 2006). This is not because they are not important contributions (far from it) or that these functions do not deserve attention, but rather that they cannot be easily recalibrated and reapplied to the more instrumental dimensions of policy design thinking. Let us now turn to those dimensions directly by asking what the inquiry can produce in relation to the many practical challenges of policy design.

2.2 The Value of the Inquiry to the Policy Designer

Having set out our focus, we now turn to showing how the study of inquiries and policy design can produce benefits. In this section, we introduce four broad categories of function through which we will study all the varying ways in which inquiries can assist the policy designer. These categories tell us that the value of the public inquiry primarily rests upon the way in which it can open up reform pathways and possibilities in the first instance (the catalytic function), the way in which it can generate support for policy action and objects (the legitimation function), the way in which it can deliver data and analysis about policy tools and causal assumptions (the learning function) and the way in which it delineates recommendations about the specific minutiae of policy processes and policy architecture (the processual function). We discuss these categories in more detail in Section 3. We also make the case here that all these functions can be captured analytically by the definition of inquiries as *procedural policy tools* (Stark and Yates 2021).

Central to all the functions delineated above is the lesson-learning role. We need not labour to explain how inquiries play a role in relation to policy learning: they generate information, craft it into evidence and then translate that into the production of action-orientated lessons which are used as advice for decision makers. Evidence and advice therefore represent *the* products of a design relevant inquiry. This places the learning function at the centre of an inquiry's relevance (Stark 2018) and tells us that the other functions noted above, and the different effects they produce, emerge through the learning function. For example, the willingness of an inquiry to use authoritative procedures to generate evidence, and an openness to public participation as a means of learning, might both give an inquiry a legitimacy that few other policy analysis mechanisms can hope to enjoy. This means that they offer the policy designer a significant legitimation stamp that can, for example, bring disparate actors to the design table to collaborate or provide support for specific objectives, causal solutions, programmes or policy tools that have not enjoyed support in the past. Regardless of the form, these legitimating benefits emerge from the fact that inquiries learn their lessons in ways that are different to the norm of policymaking.

Clearly, inquiries can be important to policy design. However, when discussing their importance, we need to continually remind ourselves that they are only advisory bodies, which means that the main game of policy choice and implementation is played elsewhere, usually at a time when the inquiry no longer exists. This has implications for how we conceptualise all the functions discussed above. We need terms that recognise that inquiries can have influence over policy change, but not directly. Thankfully pre-existing classifications can take us some of the way towards where we need to be in this regard. This is because, in the language of policy design and tools, inquiries can be understood to produce functions that make them 'procedural' rather than 'substantive' (Stark and Yates 2021). While a substantive tool directly impacts on citizens and tends to be thought of as the central component of a policy's design, procedural tools exist instead to perform a range of ancillary functions around their substantive counterpart (Bali et al. 2021). These might relate to data generation and policy analysis, coordination, implementation routes, or compliance for example. This does not mean that they are weak institutions that are not capable of producing transformative outputs. As we shall demonstrate, this is certainly not the case (Stark 2018). What it does mean, however, is that inquiries produce their effects *indirectly* by affecting the 'rules of the game' that others play rather than directly changing behaviour through the production and delivery of goods and services (Howlett 2000). Thus, in our previous work we have stated that a conceptualisation of the procedural policy tool:

> ... sits comfortably with certain features of the public inquiry, the most obvious being that they are advisory bodies without any capacity to affect citizens via the production of policy. As inquiries cannot change anything, their entire focus can be construed as an effort to indirectly influence the political and policy behaviour of others. In this sense they are very much procedural policy tools, indirectly trying to affect the nature of substantive policy created elsewhere. (Stark and Yates 2021: 350)

It is a mistake, however, to view the inquiry as a mere bit part player that cannot have a substantial role in policy change. One of the reasons that inquiries are so different to the norm of everyday policymaking relates to the fact that they often have to learn lessons about significant issues which have either been caused or addressed poorly through 'normal' policymaking endeavours. Consequently, fresh eyes, independent thinking, external voices, independent authority and an expanded timeframe for deliberation are all brought to bear on an issue with the added pressure of a public spotlight. These characteristics can mean that inquiries act as a catalyst that shakes policy out of its institutional grooves, punctuates equilibria and clears the way for a new policy path (Resodihardjo 2006). This capacity may well represent the most significant function that an inquiry can perform given what we know about the sheer extent of inertia, gradualism and incrementalism in policy change (Lindblom 1959; Pierson 2000; Mahoney and Thelen 2010). The fact that inquiries occasionally – and it is only occasionally – soften a policy space in ways that can facilitate 'first order' change (Hall 1993) can be meaningful for policy designers seeking to innovate and break from the moulds of business as usual. This might be particularly relevant, for example, when seeking to push away from incrementalism as a means of addressing wicked problems (a strategy discussed in detail by Head 2022).

We discuss this function in greater detail in the following section but what it means theoretically is that inquiries do not always conform to the typical view of a procedural policy tool. Instead, for analytical purposes, it is far better to evaluate the nature of inquiries as procedural tools by placing them onto a spectrum. At one end, we would see those rare inquiries which encourage catalytic and transformative effects, and at the other end would be inquiries which produce more typical procedural effects, which would be ancillary in nature (Stark and Yates 2021). This echoes pre-existing work on the policy change encouraged by public inquiries, which has typified inquiry outcomes into several categories from marginal to transformative (Inwood and Johns 2014: 47 and 292). However, the variable which shifts the needle from one end of the spectrum to the other, we argue, is the degree to which either the executive or the inquiry itself *controls* its functioning and outcomes. It is control, ultimately, that defines a tool in onto-logical terms. To be picked up and used presupposes that a user (in this case, the executive) can control a tool. It needs to be controlled with intentionality so that a desired outcome can be pursued. Policy tools are no different. However, inquiries represent independent entities which are meant to control themselves, and the history of those inquiries which have tended to transform policy suggests that autonomy and a willingness to do things differently was a key feature of their success (Stark 2018; Stark and Yates 2021). Therefore, when the control dial is turned towards executive sponsors, an inquiry is likely to produce typical proced-ural policy tool outputs. When the dial is swung towards inquiry independence and agency, more atypical and substantive outputs can materialise (Stark and Yates 2021), and the inquiry has more transformative potential as a policy design tool. The importance of control in relation to the public inquiry-policy design relationship leads us to reiterate Hesstvedt and Christensen's (2023: 342) conclu-sion that we need to know much more about the ways in which executives seek to control the knowledge that emerges through twenty-first century commissions of inquiry.

2.3 The Problem within Inquiries: Control, Complexity and Time

Clearly, inquiries can perform functions which policy designers can benefit from. Yet they are often convened reluctantly. Several reasons explain this reluctance. The most significant issue relates to what we have discussed immediately above – control. There are many instances in which inquiries have shown that they are not mere props to be used in the theatre of politics. Inquiry chairs have stretched their terms of reference, asked tough questions and delivered damning reports or demanding recommendations. In other words, you may not get what you asked for when you convene a powerful and independent mechanism to deliver your policy analysis and advice (Stark and Yates 2021). Moreover, the choice of whether to convene an inquiry is often taken away from executives. In many cases, inquiries are forced upon executives by political pressure or appointed by them because of a perception that they need to be used to avoid blame or survive politically (Sulitzeanu-Kenan 2010). Inquiries convened in such contexts are far removed from the concept of a policy design tool, and their functioning and advice may be seen as an imposition. What tends to happen in these contexts is that executives reassert their control after inquiries have reported by shelving or half-heartedly implementing their recommendations.

A second issue for any would-be inquiry user to think about is complexity. Here, the designer is on safer ground as this is a familiar problem. Yet the complexity involved in using an inquiry typically relates to process. For example, in order to get the most out of an inquiry's lesson learning capacity it needs to be used as part of a constellation of efforts shared across different agencies who perform a variety of tasks. In any learning episode, multiple actors will co-constitute evidence, transfer lessons once they are generated and then implement and institutionalise them across time. If these component parts are not understood as an interconnected whole, then the policy learning enterprise – the core function through which all design outputs materialise – is likely to produce sub-optimal outcomes (Stark 2020). This task is made harder by the fact that the range of actors who have authority to pursue their interests through an inquiry will change depending on its nature and the larger setting within which they operate. Some inquiries reflect the typical view that politicians are driving from the backseat while others put experts in the driving seat. Policy reviews may privilege the bureaucrat, especially if they fly under the public's radar, but when inquiries are very public, interest groups and advocacy coalitions may have much more influence. Thus, contrary to some views, inquiries are *not* simple mechanisms. They are comprised of many moving parts which can collide or complement each other. This complexity grows, moreover, as the task shifts from generating knowledge through an inquiry to implementing its recommendations. Even if goodwill exists in this regard, recommendations from an inquiry typically need to 'travel' across many different agencies who will have little obligation to implement. In such situations, learning becomes more about persuasion and incentivisation in inter-organisational settings. Complexity therefore is a standard feature of knowledge creation and recommendation delivery.

Finally, like policy design itself, the use of an inquiry needs to be located within a temporal process in which different outputs appear and disappear longitudinally. Quite simply, inquiries take time. They take time to report, and they take time to implement. Critics often point to this feature of inquiries as enabling governments to put politically difficult issues to one side, but conversely this temporal dimension can improve the policy design potential of inquiries when compared to the short-term pressures on the parts of government more usually concerned with policy design (Johns and Inwood 2018). While they face increased public scrutiny, inquiries have the (comparative) luxury of time to consider and design for effective outcomes. Subsequently, implementation and outcomes in particular often have to be measured in terms of years or even decades when it comes to inquiries. This dimension of inquiry functioning, however, is often ignored because of their temporary nature. As they blink in and out of existence, it is tempting to view them as mechanisms that only produce when the inquiry room is functioning and in the spotlight. Yet, the reality is that to be effective, inquiries need to be championed in the months and years after they have delivered their reports and wound themselves down. For scholars interested in the policy effects of inquiries, the issue of time demands longitudinal analytical frameworks that can properly acknowledge changes that may occur across longer timeframes (see, e.g., Inwood and Johns 2014: 46). For practitioners, the long-term nature of inquiry implementation demands that attention be given to issues of institutionalisation and memory retention, which we know is an issue for policy actors and public sectors generally (Pollitt 2009). Thus, the convening of an inquiry often needs to be accompanied by a long-term commitment to a reform agenda that might span across a long period of time.

2.4 The Value of the Inquiry to the Policy Design Scholar

Analysing inquiries as policy tools also offers benefits for those who study policy design. As Peters et al. (2018: 16) note in their framing of design literature, a key concern of researchers is to find and explore new 'design spaces' which can deliver effectiveness. Inquiries certainly represent one such space although, as we have discussed, their effectiveness is subject to variance.

That variance should encourage further analysis rather than preclude it however, and there are reasons to believe that reflecting on the inquiry as a design space would deliver theoretical and analytical gains. This value, we argue, emerges because, on one hand, there are so many similarities between policy design and public inquiry goals, and because, on the other hand, inquiries are so very different from 'normal' policymaking in terms of their processes and institutional context.

When thinking about similarities we can initially return to the definition of policy design given above, which emphasised it as a practice involving 'the application of knowledge about policy means gained from experience, and reason, to the development and adoption of courses of action' (Howlett 2011: 22). It is hard to think of a better definition of the analytical function performed by the public inquiry in relation to public policy, and the fact that a policy design definition can be used to define an inquiry speaks directly to the ways in which these two dimensions of scholarship are related. Other similarities exist. Consider, for example, one of the better works on the topic of policy learning, which defined it as an exercise in developing lessons about 'the viability of policy instruments or implementation designs ... [and] the social construction of policy problems, the scope of policy, or policy goals' (May 1992: 332). The parallels with this definition and the three questions that define policy design research (as discussed above) are quite remarkable. What this tells us is that inquiry lesson learning and policy design practices are largely synonymous (compare, e.g., May 1991, 1992). Therefore, the inquiry offers the policy design scholar a novel lens through which they can analyse familiar design activities in a very different set of analytical registers. We therefore argue that policy design scholars can benefit greatly from observing the operation of typical tasks in the very different context of the inquiry setting. What are those differences?

The differences between inquiry practice and design practice primarily relate to political context, institutional architecture, constituencies of interest, and knowledge transfer. When it comes to context, for example, the work of the policy official and that of the public inquiry official are very different. Typical policy work is done without much fanfare and tends to follow the logic of public management and the pace of bureaucratic life. Inquiries can be very different in all these regards. They are often accompanied by a significant amount of media attention and debate and many inquiries conduct a great deal of their business publicly. They also need to deliver reports under significant time pressure and are usually given very tight deadlines, particularly in relation to interim reports. Moreover, there is often a huge amount of expectation accompanying inquiries, especially when they are convened by governments who have a genuine need to show reform and (re)establish legitimacy. Thus, policy design scholars have an interesting opportunity to use inquiries as a means of studying policy design in public, politicised and energised contexts.

Perhaps the most obvious difference, however, is the way in which inquiries generate evidence, which means their institutional architecture can be very different from what one might find within a typical policy unit or government department. The key point of difference in this regard is of course the quasi-courtroom setting, which is not something that is typically used to generate policy advice. This dimension of the inquiry is often dismissed by those interested in policy because of its adversarial character, which in some contexts can undermine genuine efforts to learn lessons (Eburn and Dovers 2015; Dwyer 2021). Others argue that the public questioning of policy actors and the forensic reconstruction of history through the witness box can offer valuable insights into public policy that are not achievable by other means (Stark 2018). However, the issues with generating evidence solely through legal means has meant that most inquiries today surround the inquiry room with more typical forms of research, policy analysis and, at times, participatory measures that go beyond the standard call for public submissions. Therefore, the policy design scholar has a chance to observe the formulation of evidence and the generation of policy advice within a complex mechanism that is likely to have many moving parts and a variety of actors who will bring different methodological and professional preferences to the analytical table. In such contexts, the process of lesson-learning demands coordination between actors and logics and a synthesis in terms of evidence gathering and knowledge production. This complexity and the need to cohere policy advice through a collage of different actors and logics ought to be of interest to those who study the policy formulation process.

Another significant difference relates to the variety of audiences interested in an inquiry's findings. This issue ensures that the nature of knowledge production and the subsequent delivery of advice plays out quite differently through an inquiry than it does inside government. The issue of multiple audiences is significant. When government is designing policy, the formulation process tends to be private and, while analysis and advice might be published and interests consulted, the government decision maker tends to be the sole consumer of policy advice. This is also the case in relation to an inquiry report, but a key difference is that many more constituencies of interest are waiting to see the content and recommendations created by an inquiry. This creates tensions in the process of evidence generation and its translation into consumable knowledge as inquiries get pulled in different directions. Sometimes, for example, they will seek to privilege those who have been affected by the topic they are investigating. This might mean the representation of victims through testimony and report writing or the questioning of those who need to account for their actions and/or commit to subsequent action. At other times, the audience will be those who will need to implement their recommendations. Accommodating this group might mean co-constituting knowledge with policy actors through inquiry processes, shaping the content of recommendations in ways which reflect their policy preferences, and communicating in the language of policy and public management. A third audience are the advocacy coalitions that are likely to have a stake in an inquiry's conclusions, and who will certainly have a bearing on the politics surrounding the policy advice being published. Here again the design scholar has an opportunity to study how the existence of a variety of audiences affects the generation of evidence and its crafting into the knowledge and advice.

Finally, a key difference between an inquiry and a typical process of policy design relates to the way in which inquiry advice transfers around public agencies once the inquiry has shut up shop. This means that there is a need for the content and advice of a report to persuade implementing agencies when the inquiry no longer has a voice. It is of course naïve to suggest that evidence speaks for itself and that typical forms of policy advice do not attempt to persuade. However, the challenge is far greater for inquiry staff. They need to persuade reluctant implementers to act in the first place, then convince them about how to act, and they must hope that these actors have the will to institutionalise their advice over the longer term. We know from studying the implementation of public inquiries that this will is not always there and that bureaucratic and executive actors have a repertoire of measures through which they can avoid acting on inquiry reports (Brown and Stark 2022). Public inquiries therefore represent mechanisms which are just as much about advocacy as they are analysis, and inquirers that do not understand the need to convince others to act are likely to see their recommendations gathering dust on a shelf. Conversely, effective inquiries are those that prospectively consider the ways in which their advice will transfer around a variety of environments and agencies who have the power to dismiss it (Stark and Yates 2021). We return to this key theme of designing for implementation in Section 4. This challenge once again sets inquiries apart from typical design mechanisms, which tend to be convened with support from government. Thus, while the objective remains the same – deliver analysis and advice to government – the challenge is significantly harder for inquiries as they have no guarantee of support. Once again, this opens up an opportunity for design scholars to observe something different both in terms of action (designing advice that can persuade across time) and process (which will involve many more stages and actors than is typical in policy formulation). In all of these regards, the public inquiry represents an interesting policy design space, which we argue deserves further attention.

2.5 The Value of Policy Design to the Public Inquiry

Having spent some time thinking about the value of the public inquiry in relation to policy design, let us now consider the opposite. For practitioners interested in how to design and administer an effective inquiry, policy design has a lot to offer. Policy designers, for example, regularly address the challenge of public participation in the formulation of policy, and design research has much to say on this topic (Stark and Yates 2021; Saguin and Cashore 2022). Issues relating to big data, datafication and alternative forms of data for policy making are also a core concern (Hillgren et al. 2020; Maffei et al. 2020), as are the processes of lesson-drawing (or 'pinching') from overseas jurisdictions (Schneider and Ingram 1988; Rose 1991) and inviting in innovation to evidence gathering (Wellstead et al. 2021). All of these practices and the scholarship surrounding them can speak directly to the design and functioning of a public inquiry and they can therefore be used when thinking about the difficult design choices that need to be made to shape the architecture of a public inquiry (see Mulgan et al. 2021; Meyer et al. 2020; Stark and Le 2022). These benefits once again reflect the similar nature of both concerns.

However, the most important contribution that a design perspective can offer those who are involved in public inquiries relates to the selection of policy tools. Public inquiries need to structure the problems they are trying to investigate and then understand the assumptions behind policy options and the various ways in which different policy tools might offer remedies to those problems. This is where design thinking comes into its own – first, because it very much lends itself to thinking about how problems are structured and target populations are constructed (Schneider and Ingram 1993; Hoppe 2018) and second, because it is always focused on matching tools to those problems. This means policy design thinking can help inquiries to identify the causal mechanisms underneath policy (Capano and Howlett 2022), understand the need for congruence between a variety of tools in a policy mix and the different stages of policy (Howlett 2009; Hudson et al. 2019), or simply equip them with a menu of tools and a sense of the contexts that they can be applied within (Salamon 2001). This could help improve the sophistication of recommendations, which is an issue we return to in Section 4 when we discuss design effectiveness in relation to inquiry architecture.

For public inquiry scholars, there is also a lot to be gained from some of the research noted above. The most obvious gain is that inquiry researchers can use design thinking to better understand the reasons why inquiries often succeed or fail when it comes to implementation and reform. This is still an area in which scholarship has not made significant strides (Stark et al. 2023) and there is still a tendency to research inquiries as standalone entities which are disconnected from the actions which follow the publication of their reports. This is problematic in explanatory terms as success or failure evaluations need to connect what happens in an inquiry to how it is or is not supported subsequently. It is also problematic normatively as arguments about improvement need to properly understand why inquiries get shelved. One significant reason for shelving that remains under-acknowledged, for example, is that inquiries often fail to appreciate how policy is designed and implemented (House of Commons 2005; Stark 2020).

Finally, design scholarship can help us better conceptualise the complex processes that constitute inquiry learning, knowledge production and advice giving. Design literature is characterised by a comprehensive effort to define, classify and typify the components through which policy is formulated and the process through which it is understood, shaped and delivered for implementation (for overviews, see Bali et al. 2019; Capano and Howlett 2020; Mukherjee et al. 2021). These efforts provide a conceptual vocabulary that could be applied to better understanding the complex process that inquiry knowledge follows. This would benefit inquiry scholarship, in which the inquiry is all too often defined as a standalone mechanism that has a limited role. Such views stymie the development of knowledge about them by underplaying the complexity of elements in a policy-learning episode, the number of actors required, and the bricolage involved in knowledge production. Design scholarship, however, has been getting to grips with these characteristics by systematically mapping and defining them in relation to public policy. This process could also be applied to inquiry analysis so that complexity could be brought into analytical focus and properly understood. However, perhaps the greatest benefit that it might deliver would be an answer to the problem of fragmentation, discussed in Section 1, which characterises inquiry literature at the moment.

If these benefits are to materialise, it will be via the work of scholars who see value in making the effort to think about inquiries as procedural policy tools that are relevant to policy design processes. Section 3 shows this relevance in empirical terms by working through many examples of inquiries acting as procedural policy tools in ways which produce policy outcomes.

3 What Can Inquiries Offer the Policy Designer?

Thus far, our discussion has been rather theoretical in nature. However, the literature on inquiries offers a rich stream of international examples, which we use here to discuss the four functions that allow us to claim that inquiries are procedural policy tools. First, the *catalytic function* – the ability to deliver kinetic energy to lethargic or path dependent policy areas. Second, the *learning function* – the ability to deliver a variety of analyses and, consequently, a range of policy learning outcomes. Third, the *processual function* – the ability to deliver blue-prints which structure the minutiae of policy procedure and governance architecture. Fourth, the *legitimation function* – the ability to deliver support and credibility to policy reform via the use of participatory forms of policy analysis. These four functions represent the ways in which public inquiries perform as procedural policy tools. We turn to each of them below.

3.1 The Catalytic Function

Public inquiries can be instruments which propel movement in policy terms. This is an important capacity because decades of research has shown us that policy dynamics can often be pedestrian in terms of pace and that transformative policy change is often unlikely. We know, for example, that some policies remain path dependent because changes to the status quo are inconceivable to policy actors (Kay 2006). In other areas, the need to reform is recognised but efforts to change stall because institutions and interests are intransigent (Pierson 2000). However, even in those policy areas in which actors and institutions are said to be in constant flux, the pace of change often appears glacial, and the scale of change gets described through the language of incrementalism (Streeck and Thelen 2005). Public inquiries, however, can create kinetic energy that prompts and sustains policy motion.

We see this function in a range of inquiry related research endeavours. Inquiries are often an empirical feature in accounts of change, for example, which emphasise critical junctures and punctuated equilibria as the initial propellant of change (Stark 2018). However, beyond these generative moments, inquiries have also shown a capacity to deliver impetus to pre-existing ideas and policy solutions so that they are viewed as policy options that ought to be made sustainable (Herweg 2016). Comparative inquiry research has also shown how the ability of inquiries to generate consensus between interests can be an important means of prompting policy change for governments that have a weak degree of electoral support (Hesstvedt and Christiansen 2022: 448). Finally, inquiries can also champion the need for change across time in ways which ensure that actors stay on the path of reform when the journey becomes gruelling (Parker and Dekker 2008). We therefore use the term *catalytic function* as a means of describing these benefits, which are all centred around the *capacity of inquiries to propel motion and movement within policy areas.* Given the inertia typically ascribed to policy processes, this function might be one of the most important that an inquiry can offer a policy designer.

In this section, we are interested in giving international examples of each inquiry function. Let us therefore begin with an excellent illustration of the catalytic function in action. In 2013, legislation was passed to create a National Disability Insurance Scheme (NDIS) in Australia. The policy was fully implemented in 2020 and the NDIS now delivers more than $30 billion of funding to over half a million Australian citizens who have a permanent or significant disability so that they can purchase their own support. The policy delivers a form of social insurance that is funded entirely through public expenditure. It is not means-tested, and funds are allocated directly to service users. While it must be acknowledged that implementation of this landmark reform has been beset with difficulties, its design features have led to the NDIS being described as 'a path-breaking reform of disability support services in Australia' (Thill 2015: 16) and 'the most fundamental social policy reform since the introduction of Medicare' (Walsh and Johnson 2013). A notable feature of the NDIS's creation is that it was approved with bi-partisan support from the major parties in Australia, despite entering the federal Parliament during a period that was characterised by an extreme style of adversarial politics within and across those parties (Needham and Dickinson 2018).

Central to this policy design and development success was the momentum provided by a Productivity Commission inquiry which reported in 2011 (Buckmaster and Clark 2018). This inquiry determined that the system of disability funding was broken and that most Australian families could not adequately prepare for the risk and financial impact of significant disability. It proposed an NDIS and set out economic modelling to support its recommendations. Many commentators have recognised the importance of this inquiry in the story of the NDIS's creation (e.g., Carey et al. 2018; Buckmaster and Clark 2018; Needham and Dickinson 2018) and it has been praised as a momentum generating mechanism because of several features. First, it was a means through which the voices of people with disability were communicated to government (Thill 2015: 21). Second, it has been argued that this inquiry dampened potential political objections, particularly around cost, through the delivery of robust evidence that emphatically showed the need for urgent change (Walsh and Johnson 2013: 333). Third, the design of the NDIS synthesises aspects of market and state as it empowers service users to control their own spending and engage in market choice, but still resides within a social insurance model that is delivered by government (Carey et al. 2018). This design allowed the NDIS to speak to both sides of the ideological debate in Australia. In all of these ways, this inquiry was very much a mechanism that played a role in the *shaping of the problem definition* and the subsequent solution. This capacity is what gives an inquiry its catalytic potential.

The 9/11 Commission represents a second well-known example through which we can develop our understanding of this function. Indeed, this inquiry's work has been described as 'a catalyst for the landmark legislation to reform the U.S. intelligence community' (Falkenrath 2004: 188). That landmark legislation was The Intelligence Reform and Terrorism Prevention Act, which established the Director of National Intelligence, the National Counterterrorism Center, the Privacy and Civil Liberties Oversight Board, and a widescale reorganisation of anti-terrorism policy in the United States. It is tempting to see the events that prompted this Commission as so consequential that reform was inevitable. However, as Parker and Dekker's (2008: 259) analysis of the Commission's success notes, '[i]n light of the Pentagon's fierce opposition and the White House's ambivalence towards the bill, the intelligence reform act would have likely been derailed and defeated if not for the strong backing of the 9/11 Commission'.

However, unlike the Productivity Commission example above, it was not the nature of the evidence or the lessons themselves that energised the case for change here. Indeed, while the analysis performed by the Commission was praised, its connection with the lessons the Commission generated was actually questioned (Posner 2005). What Parker and Dekker show, however, is that the Commission acted as a catalyst by 'achieving the status of a trusted interpretative authority' (Parker and Dekker 2008: 274). It did this through a strategy of communication which made it the author of *the* authoritative account of events. Subsequently, its recommendations shared that authority. That communication strategy had several features. First, the Commission consistently communicated its neutrality in the face of political pressure and refused to assign blame to individuals even when it became embroiled in public disputes over access to evidence. Second, it delivered an award winning and widely accessible report which was written in a way that was designed to 'transcend the passions of the moment' (May 2005). Third, the ten Commissioners from the inquiry created the 9/11 Public Discourse Project to champion their work for some time after the inquiry ended. These features allowed the Commission to succeed in the contest over meaning making and it was this success which meant it was a catalyst for the specific policy design that followed.

Other inquiry scholarship makes similar claims about the effects that can be produced from an inquiry that becomes an interpretative authority (Chapman 1973; Resodihardjo 2006). For example, Resodihardjo (2006) analyses the ground-breaking changes in criminal justice policy that followed the Woolf Inquiry in the United Kingdom. That inquiry was similar to the 9/11 Commission in that it too became known as *the* interpretative authority on the issue of prison reform and, also like the 9/11 Commission, it provided the impetus for policy change because of the way in which it shaped public debate. This influence created a new problem definition that began the shift away from a punitive to a rehabilitative criminal justice regime. This led Resodihardjo (2006: 204) to use the term catalyst when speaking about the Woolf Inquiry. The lineage of the term, however, stretches back to Vickers's (1965: 50) classic work on decision making, which subsequently influenced Chapman's (1973) analysis of royal commissions. In this latter work, Chapman (1973: 186–7) noted how commissions are 'not only analytic but catalytic' because:

> One of the values of a commission – at least in the opinion of those sympathetic to reforms within the system of government – is to give a push to the official bureaucracy to begin reform activities. This is done partly in the specific recommendations that may be contained in the report, but perhaps more importantly, by breaking the ice so that changes, including those not previously mentioned at all, become discussable. Thus commissions not only have the role of appreciating a situation, they also on occasions create a climate for action.

We now have a pattern in our examples that underscores how inquiries propel action by redefining problems and solutions, attracting support for both and encouraging climates for new thinking and action. Ultimately, this is what makes them catalytic policy design tools (Stark and Yates 2021). While this is a common thread that connects our examples, it is important to emphasise that the direction of change need not necessarily fulfil the wishes of policy designers. Momentum for change can also be taken away from a policy's development because of an inquiry's work. This is often the case, for example, when inquiries are invited to conduct environmental impact assessments or to evaluate the value of large-scale infrastructure projects. In these cases, change comes through rejection and dynamics look different. Yet these inquiries are still catalytic. Consider, for example, the Inquiry into the Construction of a Pipeline in the Mackenzie Valley (the Berger Inquiry). In the short term, this inquiry prevented a series of policies from proceeding and ensured that one large resource extractor's project would not damage Canada's northern environment or its Indigenous communities. This might not seem particularly catalytic. However, this inquiry has gone down in Canadian history as a 'game changer' that has managed to redefine settler-Indigenous, market and state and north and south relations (Abele 2014). The short and the long term have been well described by one of the inquiry's staff:

> With the publication of volume 1, the dye was cast. The Arctic Gas proposal would simply never proceed, and the north slope of the continent would remain undamaged. Many royal commission reports have profoundly

affected Canadian public policy. This report not only did that, but it did so by reversing the direction in which the federal government wished to move. It did so, very simply, by the unanswerably powerful case it presented. (Goudge 2016: 402)

Indeed, in the words of one analysis, this was an inquiry that has 'established an enduring paradigm for public understanding of the meaning of northern development' (Abele 2014: 88). It did so by mobilising a new set of actors, ideas and relationships that completely redefined the nature of the policy design challenge (Abele 2014: 102–5).

Before moving on it is worth underscoring just how different the catalytic function is here in relation to more typical policy design processes. As discussed above, this difference comes through the very political setting in which problem definition and policy framing play out. In each example, there is a public contest around the capacity to define problems and solutions and set the general direction of policy travel. Moreover, these inquiries were successful catalysts because each managed to 'win' over constituencies of interest through effective public communication. Each inquiry was certainly different in terms of how they played that game. In the case of the Productivity Commission strict expertise and impartiality were the order of the day while for the 9/11 Commission and the Berger Inquiry, advocacy and politics had to be played. Nevertheless, the common thread is that each influenced the public and political debate to such an extent that they became catalysts for change. This is a policy design function but not as we know it.

3.2 The Learning Function

Every inquiry produces knowledge but not all inquiries are about learning. The public act of asking questions, generating evidence and publishing recommendations can look like learning is going on but as we have discussed, inquiries can actually be about something else: the delivery of accountability or blame, the re-legitimation of the status quo or the substantiation of pre-existing policy positions, for example. Let us therefore begin our discussion here with a clear definition of policy learning and a subsequent definition of what that means in relation to public inquiries.

The easiest way to define policy learning is through the process that produces it. Learning begins with the individual and can therefore be defined initially as 'the updating of beliefs based on lived or witnessed experiences, analysis or social interaction' (Dunlop and Radaelli 2013: 599). We get to *policy* learning from here via two steps. The first step links cognitive change at the individual level to collective change at the organisational level. This is important as policymaking is a collective endeavour. The second processual step connects collective learning to outputs which might facilitate behavioural, value-orientated, or further cognitive change (Stark 2019). While the range of outputs that can materialise from a learning process is limitless, the key to defining the existence of policy learning rests in an ability to observe the links between individual and collective learning and specific policy changes. This is important because if those links are not established, one could be observing change but not necessarily learning-induced change.

Policy learning via public inquiry follows a similar but not identical process. As all learning begins with the individual, we will initially see individual cognitive change and updated beliefs within an inquiry. Once again, this needs to become collective and the inquiry (or at least key figures within it) will need to translate that individual learning into a shared lesson (usually in the form of a recommendation). A key difference in the causal process, however, stems from the fact that inquiries cannot implement their own lessons. They need to encourage others to learn about their learnings, buy into them and then produce the outputs on their behalf. This means that inquiry induced policy learning also requires an additional round of inter-organisational learning that involves a larger collection of implementing actors. Thus, to show inquiry induced policy learning, we need to connect an inquiry that has learned, to an implementer that has learned that inquiry lesson, to a policy change that they have put in place because of that process. Once those links have been established researchers can use the wide array of typologies and concepts found in the policy learning literature to characterise the nature of the learning that they observe (for a good overview here, see Dunlop and Radaelli 2021).

However, there are many cases in which it is impossible to make these connections. The reasons for this disconnect are well canvassed above and below this discussion but they can be reduced to an essential point, which is that we will only see policy learning when an inquiry's members are motivated by a genuine belief in the need for learning and when its sponsors have a genuine commitment to the actioning of lessons. Nevertheless, certain types of inquiries seem to produce more learning outputs than others. For example, we often see policy learning in *problem-solving, post-crisis* and *emergent technology* inquiries. These kinds of inquiries give us an insight into how the learning function can be deployed in policy design terms.

According to Hunter and Boswell (2015: 13), *problem-solving commissions* can be distinguished from inquiries that seek to establish legitimation or substantiate pre-existing positions. This is because they are convened when 'the agency establishing the commission recognises it has gaps in its knowledge, and considers that a commission will be an appropriate means for delivering the required expertise or evidence'. Such a description suggests a rather circumscribed form of policy learning, particularly as these authors are keen to emphasise that inquiries can produce good effects when they 'have understood and embraced the priorities and objectives of policymakers, and see their job as further developing policy along those lines' (Hunter and Boswell 2015: 23). However, in their analysis, they discuss a specific case in which one inquiry performed this role in relation to integration policy in the United Kingdom. This inquiry – The Community Cohesion Review Team – did so by elaborating the concept of community cohesion to such an extent that it encouraged a paradigm shift in policy thinking and, simultaneously, produced lessons that propelled the implementation of several important recommendations. The result was a policy change that shifted the values and instruments of integration policy in ways that allowed it to go beyond a focus on multicultural differences.

While the example above shows us that big things can come from narrow learning remits, sometimes the policy learning function is turned to in order to produce big ideas. Often this is the case when policy actors simply do not have an answer to a new problem or when an intractable issue has remained despite several attempts to address it. In the Nordic countries, the system of public inquiry commissions and committees has been described as a 'cornerstone' of policy development (Hesstvedt and Christiansen 2022). In this tradition, the Finnish 'future school task force' was appointed to investigate the reasons behind declining educational outcomes and to make recommendations around a vision of 'the school of the future'. While several such inquiries occurred in Nordic countries during a similar period, this task force brought together a large group of actors from a variety of organisations and sectors to reframe the very idea of schooling (Hansen et al. 2021). The task force report frames school education as something to be reinvented on a continuous basis and suggests that schools ought to become test laboratories for the latest technology and that they ought to partner with industry to encourage entrepreneurial skills. Amongst other things, the report also emphasised that school days should be more flexible rather than tightly scheduled and that much more student 'voice and choice' was required (Ministry of Education and Culture 2015; Hansen et al. 2021). These big ideas challenged the status quo and encouraged public debate and social learning about the fundamentals of the education system.

Alongside problem-solving inquiries are those which are convened to learn about emergent technologies that are viewed as important but not well understood. These can often prompt learning which encourages changes because they perform a *sensemaking function* in moments of uncertainty. For example, the Royal Commission on New Reproductive Technologies was convened in Canada to investigate the 'social, ethical, health, research, legal and economic

implications' of emerging IVF treatments. This Commission, which was characterised by conflict between its members (see Scala 2014), still managed to
produce recommendations which led to impactful programmatic changes via
the Assisted Human Reproduction Act, the establishment of a national regulatory agency, and the extension of infertility treatments to all Canadians regardless of marital status and sexual orientation.

The emergence of nuclear power provides us with a similar story about the
influence that inquiries can have through their learning capacity. In the United
Kingdom, successive inquiries into nuclear energy produced narrow forms of
'instrumental policy learning' (Rough 2011). This type of learning leads to
policy redesigns which subsequently produce new or revised policy tools
without revising the more fundamental aspects of a policy (see May 1992). In
this case, new policy instruments allowed the government to better market and
persuade the public about its pre-established, pro-nuclear position. However, by
ensuring that learning took place at the technical-instrumental level, the inquiries prevented a meaningful public debate from taking place (Rough 2011). This
meant that instrumental learning was promoted above 'social learning'. In that
latter type of policy learning, state and society puzzle together and larger, more
value-driven change can be produced (see Heclo 1974). Similarly, Kenny and Ó
Dochartaigh (2021) argued – in relation to the 1998–2010 Saville inquiry into
the events of Bloody Sunday – that the inquiry exemplified instrumental
rationality, 'separated the political from the operational', and produced
a report narrowly framed around 'formal responsibilities and professional
competence' (p. 405). This had the direct effect of pushing responsibility
down the chain of command instead of scrutinising senior decision-makers,
and it marginalised analyses of divisions and tensions within the military that
were crucial for understanding the decision-making around Bloody Sunday. In
the nuclear power example, as the environmental lobby grew, public inquiries of
this sort became recognised as entry points and venues for a larger, more
politicised learning endeavour with the capacity to encourage public debate
(Rough 2011). Thus, the nature of policy learning changed as inquiries became
pluralist venues rather than more technical learning mechanisms.

Post-crisis inquiries also tend to encourage genuine learning and reform.
There is a tendency to think that the repeat of problematic histories, reflected in
the emergence of similar crises across time, means that no learning has taken
place in their wake. However, a great deal of learning tends to follow post-crisis
inquiries because the authorising environment is highly supportive of change
(Stark 2018). This environment encourages large amounts of instrumental
learning in the form of new policy tools designed to address the key failings
identified by inquiries. However, studies of the effects of post-crisis inquiries

have also noted how they can produce forms of organisational learning which better connect and coordinate policy actors. This outcome, which has been noted in relation to inquiries around the world, has been defined as a form of 'cognitive' organisational learning as different policy actors become aware of their place within a community of organisations who all have a shared responsibility in relation to policy (Stark 2018). In effect this form of learning creates shared interpretations across policy actors and, as a consequence, better levels of coordination. A good example of this comes from the Pitt Review in the United Kingdom, which examined significant summer flooding in 2007. That inquiry recognised that different forms of flooding were handled by disparate and disconnected agencies and that emergency flood responders and those responsible for reducing flood vulnerability across the longer term rarely coordinated. Post-inquiry, therefore, an important outcome was an increased awareness of 'others' within the policy community and an increase in coordination mechanisms that brought actors together (Stark 2018). This combination of instrumental learning and cognitive organisational learning makes post-crisis inquiries an important feature of resilience building generally.

Although the examples above are framed here in a positive light we need to be careful not to over-emphasise the extent to which inquiries produce policy learning outcomes or understate just how hard those outcomes are to produce. Looking across the cases we have discussed above we see (at least) three issues. The first is that there is a very fine line between a 'substantiating inquiry' that justifies a pre-existing position or policy direction with new learnings and an inquiry that is 'stage-managed' in order to justify a pre-existing position without any learning being considered. Indeed, while Hunter and Boswell (2015) find evidence of policy learning in one of their cases they also find a great deal of substantiating and legitimating of positions without much learning in their other cases. This substantiating dynamic is also a feature of Rough's (2011) analysis of nuclear energy learning, and it gives credence to a longer running argument that governments mobilise their bias in order to stage manage change through a process of superficial learning (see Acland 1980; Stark et al. 2023).

A second issue that can compromise policy learning in inquiries relates to the disputes that can emerge between different actors in an inquiry. These often relate to disagreements between what modes of learning or modes of knowledge production are most appropriate, and these often reflect deeper epistemological or even ideological differences between inquiry actors. In the Canadian Royal Commission on New Reproductive Technologies, for example, disputes emerged between inquiry actors who valued different forms of knowledge. Indeed, four of the commissioners filed a suit against the Commission Chair – Patricia Baird – arguing that they had not been able to participate meaningfully in several areas of the Commission's work, which undermined its aim of operating in a multidisciplinary way. These commissioners also publicly criticised what they saw as the technological and scientific bias of the research programme. In particular, Baird clashed with the sociologist Louise Vandelac due to their differing 'cognitive maps'. Scala (2014: 153) argues that the Commission's research programme and operating style supported 'a hierarchical ordering of forms of knowledge, with scientific knowledge assigned the greatest importance' and that this 'pushed to the margins the perspectives of expert and non-expert groups critical of reproductive technologies' (p. 153). This inquiry still produced learning and encouraged change, but the case shows the tensions that emerge from different rationalities all attempting to learn within a single organisation.

This kind of conflict has been noted in other inquiries. The spectacular fallout between the two chairs who led Australia's Aged Care Quality and Safety Royal Commission, for example, shows how recommendations can be undermined through a clash of personalities and professional backgrounds within an inquiry (Snape 2021). Likewise, a power struggle emerged early in the life of the 2019–2023 Australian Royal Commission into Violence, Abuse, Neglect and Exploitation of People with Disability. The Government amended the letters patent to hand unprecedented power to the Chair, who did not have a disability, at the expense of the five other commissioners (Commonwealth of Australia 2019). A former Commission staffer wrote that he 'had total control over all aspects of the Commission' (Gibbs 2022). This decision to marginalise the two Commissioners with disability – who were seen to represent (in Salter's (2007) terms) the 'disaffected public' served by the inquiry – seriously undermined the Commission's trust within the disability community.

In such examples, we see another key difference with the policy design challenge through inquiries. These mechanisms throw together different actors and logics temporarily and demand policy analysis and communication under conditions of uncertainty and pressure. This is not quite the same as a single government department working towards a policy design. Consequently, policy learning through inquiries is not merely about analysis and knowledge creation. It is also an effort in design that requires that real attention be given to *synthesising* actors and the knowledge that they produce. Typically, people are seconded to inquiries because they are successful in their specific professional realm. These actors will come into an inquiry with a pre-determined view about the nature of 'good' knowledge and the practices that produce it. This can often create conflict, which needs to be managed.

A final feature of the cases discussed above is that each inquiry produced a great deal of instrumental learning. This is certainly the dominant type of learning in post-crisis inquiries (Stark 2018) but it was also a feature of race relations inquiries in the United Kingdom (Hunter and Boswell 2015) and the nuclear power cases (Rough 2011). It is not hard to see why instrumental learning occurs. It leads to recommendations that are tangible, practical, easier to implement and run with the grain of the status quo. This means that values, norms or causal ideas are not challenged and that momentum-killing conflict is avoided. It would seem therefore that when we convene inquiries for policy learning purposes, we ought to expect lessons about policy tools rather than the theories of change or causal relationships that sit behind them. This is a valuable point for designers to consider. Inquiries may not address programme theory or the hypotheses behind policy configurations, but they can learn (and change) the instruments created by them.

Before moving on it is worth explicitly distinguishing the catalytic function and the learning function. They are related – indeed, as we have discussed, all inquiry functions emerge through an actual or ostensible relationship with the learning function. It is certainly the case therefore that agreed upon lessons produced by an inquiry can lead to catalytic change. However, catalytic and learning functions represent different categories because learning is not necessary for the catalytic function to be fulfilled (although it is likely to help). For example, there are many instances of inquiries which have not learned very effectively or not really been concerned to make learning a priority, yet they have prompted action and change merely by being convened. Thus, there is a momentum-giving element to an inquiry that can be distinct from whether, how and what it learns. This represents a clear conceptual difference between catalytic and learning outcomes as it highlights how the former can be seen when an inquiry prompts change and the latter can be seen when an inquiry prompts individual and/or collective change in cognitive or shared interpretations.

3.3 The Processual Function

As we discussed in Section 2, public inquiries can be conceptualised as procedural policy tools. What we mean by this is that they affect the rules of the game around which policy is designed without directly creating or implementing more substantive policy tools (Stark and Yates 2021). One of the clearest examples of this relates to what we are defining here as the *processual function*, which is a term we use to denote the way in which *inquiries propose very specific blueprints which can build or alter organisational and policy processes.* These blueprints typically relate to the minutiae of governance architecture that surrounds a policy and its instruments.

The focus of this function can vary in a significant manner. For example, inquiries regularly set out recommendations relating to how specific agencies should be constituted and how they should operate. This represents the archetypal example of a processual output, which is registered in small-scale changes to the architecture of an organisation. Other inquiries can be observed setting out proposals for specific mechanisms or processes relating to, for example, arbitration, redress or access to common pool resources. These are procedural in the policy tool sense as they surround the more fundamental instruments of policy delivery that affect target populations. Accountability focused inquiries often suggest processual changes too, typically because of a concern with 'good governance' which characterises their recommendations with a concern for procedural justice, equity or transparency. Regardless of the specifics of any single recommendation, what we can say is that *inquiries offer the policy designer an opportunity to create and renovate the minutiae of policy processes* in ways which can alter outcomes without necessarily changing the fundamentals. This is what we define as the processual function.

We can begin to illustrate this function with a simple example. In Australia, the Department of Environment and Heritage convened an Access Task Force in 2000. The remit given to this independent group of experts was to produce a process through which consent could be given to use Australia's natural biological resources for research. This inquiry was convened in light of post-millennial developments in genetic engineering which suggested that there was a need to establish a 'process whereby samples from individual organisms are gathered, their genetic and biochemical make-up and other attributes determined, and their potential use assessed' (ABRC 2000: 1.43). The result was the Access to Biological Resources in Commonwealth Areas Report. The Report recommended a process in which consent was to be generated in a way that respected the precautionary principle in science, the principles of sustainable development, environmental concerns and the wishes of Indigenous landowners in Australia. The inquiry proposed an access and permit scheme which included a benefit sharing contract system. This subsequently formed the basis of a nationally consistent approach, agreed upon by all the state and territory governments of Australia. This is a perfect illustration of the processual function. In an uncertain area in which decision-makers have already set the policy ends and considered the needs of relevant stakeholders, an inquiry is used to determine a specific procedure that would structure delivery of a policy process.

The processual function is often a feature of inquiries that attempt to explain wrongdoing. These inquiries tend to suggest very specific blueprints for change for two reasons. First because that is how lawyers operate – the detail of process and procedure is everything. Second, because these kinds of inquiry are calibrated towards preventing recurrences of specific types of bad behaviour. Thus, specific wrongdoing is addressed via very specific recommendations. In South Africa, for example, the State Capture Commission, led by the Chief Justice of South Africa, has investigated cases of corruption involving politicians, public servants and senior figures in state owned enterprises. Across four voluminous reports, the Commission has reported on case after case of corruption and wilful negligence but, as might be expected, its recommendations offer a very specific set of processual blueprints for reform. These include processes for the transparent and competitive appointment of senior public servants (JCISC 2022: 714), the creation of national charters and codes of conduct with 'sign off' processes to ensure third party scrutiny (p. 844), and processes that delineate how the membership and methods of funding for new watchdogs ensure impartiality (pp. 845–8). This level of specificity, which drills right down to the process for appointing and funding employees of the state, is quite typical of inquiries that seek accountability. The Leveson Inquiry in the United Kingdom, which examined the culture, practices and ethics of the press after a series of high-profile phone hacking scandals, produced similar blueprints which were meant to establish a new regulatory body (Leveson 2012: 1808–9). Leveson proposed a series of very specific process recommendations which detailed procedures for establishing the body's membership, internal governance processes, powers and sanctions and so on.

However, process recommendations need not be about the design of agencies. They can also delineate processes for specific forms of policy implementation. These recommendations represent an interesting inquiry output as they do not change the policy's design or its instruments but instead offer specific procedures that are focused on improving the architecture around delivery and implementation. Good examples here come in the form of inquiries which have examined implementation failures. Perhaps the most obvious example of this type of inquiry can be seen in those that have been convened to address failures in child protection policy. For example, Buckley and O'Nolan (2013) note that since the early 1990s there have been no fewer than 29 inquiries into child protection policy in Ireland, which have produced 551 recommendations. Like those conducted in the United Kingdom (see Elliott 2009), the recommendations of these inquiries consistently focused on procedure at the front-line in attempts to improve the 'vigilance and identification of children at risk; better interagency cooperation, record-keeping and exchange of information; and protocols for child protection conferences' (Buckley and O'Nolan 2013: 3). Underpinning many inquiries of this nature is the claim that it is delivery processes, rather than policy design, that cause repeated failures vis-à-vis child protection. These inquiries therefore focus on improving the minutiae of 'street-level' processes rather than the principles of child protection policy.

The examples above all show that there is a potential for policy formulators to use inquiries as a means of designing and delineating specific blueprints that enhance policy agencies and processes. These might, inter alia, shape the public services and human resources surrounding policy, facilitate the building of new agencies, or delineate new delivery and implementation procedures 'below' the typical features of a policy's design. We need to be careful, however, when we think about proposing process solutions generally and, more specifically, when we attempt to propose them via accountability seeking inquiries. At a general level, policy designers need to be careful to avoid implementing solutions that simply graft or bolt on new processes to existing designs. Good architectural solutions ought to work with the existing environment rather than adding incongruous or ugly features to it. This issue has also been recognised in those studies which have focused upon the moment when policy is terminated, succeeded or layered upon (deLeon 1978; Hogwood and Peters 1983; Mahoney and Thelen 2010). In relation to each, what we see is new processes and procedures being built upon the old without any active dismantling of past tools (see Bauer et al. 2012). When this occurs the literature tells us that the new synthesis can often undermine rather than improve policy performance, especially in relation to policy that needs to be adaptive. Moreover, grafting new onto old can mean that inefficient redundancies are created (see, e.g., Kay 2007). Therefore, the degree to which process recommendations complement or collide with existing policy configurations is a key concern but it is one that is regularly ignored by inquiries. Indeed, inquiries focused on accountability rather than policy learning are likely to propose processual solutions without thinking about the issues created by policy succession or layering. This, alongside the fact that the search for wrongdoing often turns off would-be implementers (Eburn and Dovers 2015), provides us with another reason why some of the inquiries above (such as the Leveson Inquiry for example) have had their processual recommendations rejected by executives.

3.4 The Participatory-Legitimation Function

Policy design studies have recently shown an interest in the potential of citizen participation in relation to policy formulation (Blomkamp 2022; De Smedt and Borch 2022; Saguin and Cashore 2022). Saguin and Cashore (2022: 2) take us to the heart of this value by identifying the two most common reasons that are given for engaging with citizens as part of a policy analysis process. The first emerges from the 'logic of consequences' which sits comfortably within the means-end thinking of the policy designer. This first rationale, they tell us, is essentially 'instrumental: that is, citizens bring tacit knowledge that improve, rather than counteract, the rationality of policy interventions'. In simpler terms, citizens provide data that enhances our understanding of policy. Experimental research in design studies has shown this to be the case by illustrating how the lived 'everyday' experience of citizens can generate novel insights about the linkages between policy and the associated configuration of policy tools that is required to get policy to them (Stark et al. (2021)).

This capacity for citizens to deliver essential data is certainly one reason why they are used in public inquiries. However, this analytical benefit is rarely discussed on the public stage when it comes to citizen participation in inquiries. Much more common are references to a different set of norms, which relate to the necessity of speaking to those who have caused or are affected by the issues the inquiry has been convened to investigate. This takes us to Saguin and Cashore's (2022: 2) second rationale for using participatory processes for policy design, which relates to March and Olsen's (1984) well-known 'logic of appropriateness'. A common claim is that participatory forms of analysis generate *legitimacy*, which in this case relates to 'legitimacy for the policy and/or the authoritative arena charged with developing, and implementing, a policy mix' (Saguin and Cashore 2022: 2). Thus, engaging with citizens and allowing them to participate in an inquiry is seen as an appropriate institutional response and consequently one which delivers a degree of legitimacy to recommendations.

The policy design literature has developed in a way that has created a distinction between these two rationales, which are said to operate in a countervailing manner (Saguin and Cashore 2022). However, in a public inquiry participation can forward both values simultaneously by delivering appropriateness and legitimacy through the generation of policy relevant data. We refer to this as the *participatory-legitimation function*.

When it comes to the first rationale – the delivery of sound data for analytical purposes – a good case study comes in the form of the Victorian Bushfires Royal Commission (VBRC) in Australia. That inquiry took an expansive view of participation and, prior to the questioning of witnesses in more formal proceedings, conducted extensive consultation work in the communities that were affected by a series of disastrous bushfires. Notably, senior figures inside the inquiry (who were unaccustomed to participatory means of this nature) validated community views as an important form of policy-relevant knowledge. Statements such as those below, for example, show that participatory dynamics were much more than 'window dressing' designed to secure public credibility. Instead, the data generated from the community:

> was absolutely fundamental in terms of shaping the inquiry's analysis. It went to what the lived experience said had been important in terms of the community's understanding ... and it helped us see that those are the things that people expect us to address. And we absolutely tested those views. This was one important input, and it was only one input, but it was a critical one because *what became apparent was that they were right.* What may not have come from researchers, may not have been academic and may not have been based in a whole load of expert data was lived experience of those things that had influenced them and what was important to understand. The community absolutely got that right, and we tested it as we went through. Yes, there were other things that were added on as we went through but that core view, it was bang on. (VBRC Official A, interview with author)

This view of the analytical worth of lived experience very much complements those emerging studies of policy design which explore citizen participation (e.g., Gouache 2022). However, there is no doubt that participatory mechanisms that include communities also generate legitimacy. This is a powerful function because when notions of appropriateness are satisfied, policy designs have an easier time when it comes to getting off the design table and into delivery strategies. This is especially true when it comes to policy areas which are politically fraught. For example, the Royal Commission of Inquiry into the Terrorist Attack on Christchurch Mosques was convened to determine what relevant state sector agencies knew about the activities of the perpetrator of the 15 March 2019 terrorist attack on the Al-Noor Mosque before the attack took place; what actions those agencies took in light of that knowledge; whether there was anything they should have done differently; and what additional measures those agencies should take in the future to prevent attacks. Clearly, this was an inquiry that was going to produce recommendations of a sensitive nature that would have implications for community cohesion. The inquiry therefore created the Muslim Community Reference Group as a means of constructively questioning and criticising aspects of its work and delivering feedback directly from and to the Muslim community. This group fed into the inquiry directly and, at the same time, delivered a very public example of the constructive and positive impact that they could make to contemporary policymaking. The visible inclusion of a mechanism that represented the wider community clearly had a legitimating effect which was recorded in positive media commentary and public views about the inquiry and its recommendations (e.g., Roy 2020).

In a similar vein, a constellation of government, non-government, lived experience and advocacy groups were crucial to the production of the landmark

Victorian Royal Commission into Family Violence report in 2016. Recognising that 'legal change without cultural change is likely to have limited effect', this inquiry's Commissioner designed its internal processes to 'bring people along with it' (Yates 2018: 113). This was crucial because most family violence and allied services are delivered by non-government organisations. Accordingly, the Commission demonstrated an openness to new ideas and ensured the inclusion of groups and actors that previously had felt excluded from these kinds of policy exercises. While the Commission was primarily focused on producing innovative policy ideas over a short timeframe, it balanced this goal with the inclusion of 'lay witnesses' who had lived experience of family violence and could frame and contextualise the testimony of the expert and practitioner witnesses at public hearings. This decision kept the focus on policy learning while recognising community expectations that the Commission would foreground the voices of victim-survivors (Yates 2018).

A third example is the Commission of Inquiry into Policing in Khayelitsha, which examined the systemic breakdown in policing in a South African township (Jain 2020). The Commission was established to make forward-looking policy recommendations rather than fact-find to bring particular actors to account. Hailed as a 'people's commission', it spent a year making connections in the local community and advertising the Commission to disseminate information as broadly as possible, working with civil society organisations to support translation and dissemination of materials and facilitate broad participation. The venue chosen for hearings was located in the township itself, in a venue that was welcoming to the public. Hearings were widely attended by media and the community. Such processes facilitated trust with both community groups and the local police; the latter were initially suspicious but eventually convinced that the inquiry intended to provide solutions rather than to assign blame. This good relationship enabled the Commission to access a high volume of policy-relevant information. Ultimately, though political struggles characterised the implementation of recommendations, the Commission was able to bridge divides and articulate a commonly accepted understanding of the problem.

What we have shown in the examples above are the specific ways in which inquiries can act as procedural policy tools. They may not directly implement policy designs or instruments, but inquiries learn about both in ways which encourage others to produce 'instrumental' policy learning outputs, which are registered in the form of subsequent policy tools. Their capacity to 'sensemake' and to offer authoritative problem definitions and solutions means that they can catalyse policy momentum when inertia is the norm. Governance architecture and policy process can be shaped by the blueprints that they recommend and, perhaps most importantly, by including citizens into meaningful policy analyses, they offer the chance for policy formulators and their designs to enjoy legitimacy and support. However, let us not forget that inquiries are idiosyncratic creatures. Some inquiries produce these effects, others produce some but not all, and some produce nothing much at all for the policy designer. This variance prompts the question: what is it that makes an inquiry effective? More specifically, what are the institutional features of an inquiry that have a bearing on its effectiveness? We now turn to these questions in Section 4.

4 Designing Effective Inquiries

We now turn to our third concern, which is how to design inquiries and associated processes to ensure their effectiveness, both in a broad sense as policy tools and as regards their policy design functions. The question of effectiveness and how inquiries might be designed to improve it is a difficult one. In this area, inquiry literature reflects the policy sciences generally in that it has much to say about failure but little to say about success (Douglas et al. 2021). Nevertheless, we can turn to the voluminous number of works that document inquiry problems and ask what they tell us about how *not* to design these mechanisms (Salter 2007; Eburn and Dovers 2015; Stark et al. 2023). We can also identify the small number of inquiries that have been labelled as a success and reflect upon what these tell us about effective institutional features (Inwood and Johns 2014; Stark 2018; Resodihardjo 2020). Finally, policy design thinking can also help us here by telling us something about the relationship between the selection of policy tools and effectiveness (Peters et al. 2018). Understanding that relationship is also important because it can help with the design of inquiry recommendations.

Consideration of all these literatures leads to the argument unfolded below, which claims that *plurality* is a fundamental variable that influences inquiry effectiveness. This argument is presented below via the development of a 3×2 typology, which tells us that: 1) methodological pluralism is essential for effective learning and knowledge creation through inquiries; 2) recommendations that are designed and communicated as 'mixes' or 'bundles' will have a better chance of addressing the complexity of the implementation stage; and 3) when a large plurality of actors are involved in the implementation process, there is less chance of inquiry success. Thus, we argue that inquiry effectiveness is significantly influenced by the extent to which an inquiry's *internal constitution, policy tool selection and implementing environment are monocentric or polycentric.* Good design choices around these three factors, we argue, separate those inquiries that are quickly forgotten from those which have an enduring influence on policy. Before we get to this argument, however, we must first define what we mean by effectiveness in this context.

4.1 New Context, Old Problems: Measuring Inquiry Effectiveness

Any evaluation of effectiveness in a policy context immediately confronts a series of issues that are well identified in the policy sciences but largely unresolved. These relate to defining and measuring effectiveness and connecting it causally to antecedent variables. More specifically, evaluations need to contend with the subjective and relative nature of effectiveness (Peters et al. 2018: 15), the fact that programmatic or policy success need not correlate with political success, which means that policy failures can be declared successes and vice versa (Bovens et al. 2001: 25), and the many ways in which rational-instrumental modes of policy analysis limit understandings of effectiveness by winnowing evaluations into technical exercises that rely on narrow indicators (Carter 1989; Sanderson 2002; Fischer 2003).

Enduring problems such as these are instructive in that they remind us that effectiveness is a slippery concept that needs to be treated with care in any evaluation. This need for care is exacerbated by the variance we see in the functioning and focus of the public inquiry. Two issues stand out in this regard. First, cognisance of the many different functions that can be performed by an inquiry is essential so that an evaluation can make judgements on appropriate criteria. For example, if an inquiry is convened to map out a blueprint for a policy that is already agreed upon (the processual function), its ability to engender large-scale policy change (the catalytic function) should not be assessed. Following on from this is a second issue which is that what an inquiry ought to be doing in functional terms is both constructed and contested by the variety of actors who are interested in it. For example, public managers interested in policy reform via an inquiry might lament the fact that it uses counsel and takes evidence via cross-examination. From their perspective, this might be a sign that the inquiry is more interested in wrongdoing than policy learning. Conversely, if an event that has led to significant loss of life or property is responded to via a policy review which does not have public proceedings, then it will be likely to be viewed as a failure by victims because of a belief that those who have created problems have been 'let off the hook'. The key point in all of this is that subjective evaluations play out through a normative lens, which is coloured by perceptions of what function an inquiry ought to perform. And because different actors hold different assumptions in this regard, evaluations of success and failure will always attach themselves to the same inquiry.

To some extent, inquiry scholarship has begun to get to grips with this complexity. This has been done by applying the literature on policy success (Bovens et al. 2001; McConnell, 2010; Compton and 't Hart 2019) to the functioning of public inquiries (see Stark 2023). Here, however, brevity demands that we sidestep some of this complexity and move forward with a definition of effectiveness which allows us to think about the essence of institutional design choices. For that reason, we have chosen to define inquiry effectiveness in two ways. First, we can say that a successful inquiry would be one which has managed to produce recommendations that have a capacity to address the problems that caused it to be convened in the first place. In methodological terms, the easiest way to make this assessment is to engage directly with would-be implementers and apposite experts and simply ask: was this an inquiry that produced valid lessons that, if implemented, could address the problem that it was convened to address? Second, a successful inquiry would be one which managed to get recommendations implemented in ways which produced outcomes that affected the issues that it was convened to address. Thus, an evaluation of inquiry success would also 'track' recommendations to determine if they were actioned and, once again, analyse associated outcomes by engaging directly with the perceptions of policy actors (e.g., see Stark et al. 2023).

4.2 Understanding Inquiry Design through Failures

When it comes to these two yardsticks, inquiry literature is generally negative. We therefore have a long list of the things that inquiries supposedly do wrong, which allows us to think about the pitfalls of institutional design. For example, some of the most enduring criticisms in relation to our first measure of effectiveness – the quality of recommendations – are that they are blighted by their adversarial nature, which undermines genuine learning (Eburn and Dovers 2015; Dwyer 2021). When this occurs the quality of the evidence that inquiries generate, and the recommendations that are based upon that evidence, are both weakened because those who give evidence become overly defensive (Stark 2018). A second criticism of inquiries is that their proceedings reflect a form of institutional conservatism that makes them slow-moving and myopic (Jenkins 2021) and unlikely to generate findings of relevance in the twenty-first century (Elliott and McGuinness 2002; Flinders et al. 2021; Stark and Le 2022). One reflection of this is the commonly voiced view that inquiry personnel (particularly chairs) are ignorant of policy process and public sector contexts and therefore produce recommendations which cannot be implemented (HC 2005; Elliot 2009; Stark 2020).

In relation to the second criterion of effectiveness set out above – the frequency of implementation and the quality of outcomes – the negative inquiry literature typically tells us that inquiries do not get regularly implemented and that outcomes are rarely forthcoming. Reasons such as those given above tend to also be cited in explanations of poor implementation. In addition, the politics of reform and blame avoidance may undermine efforts to implement inquiries (Stark et al. 2023), and recommendations may not travel or transfer across the multiplicity of different actors required for implementation (Stark 2020). Finally, the sheer complexity and challenge of implementation can prove so great that reform efforts stall and are abandoned (Brown and Stark 2022).

Each of the critical points noted above can be traced to an empirical analysis of one or more public inquiries. However, when thinking about 'how not to do it', would-be convenors and newly appointed inquiry staff can learn much from the design of twenty-first century Royal Commissions in Australia. These inquiries have often struggled to meet the criteria of effectiveness set out above. Indeed, after tracking the recommendation of every Royal Commission in Australia since 2000 (at the federal level), Stark et al. (2023: 5) concluded that a mere 37 per cent (166 of 444) of recommendations were implemented. This is of course a rather crude measurement of effectiveness, not least because variance exists within the sample: the lowest rate of implementation of one inquiry was 12 per cent while the highest was 100 per cent. Moreover, the frequency of implementation is misleading as a measure of effectiveness as it only takes one implemented recommendation to produce a substantive outcome while a hundred might only achieve superficial change. However, when policy actors connected to these inquiries were interviewed and asked to decide whether the inquiry in question prompted substantive policy outcomes, only 50 per cent of the sample received positive acknowledgment. This research therefore concluded that the extent of Royal Commission implementation in Australia was 'rather dismal' (Stark et al. 2023: 16). Mintrom et al. (2021) made similar observations in their review of Australian policy-focused royal commissions conducted in the past 50 years.

While these low rates might be concerning to the citizens of Australia, more important to our immediate concern are the reasons that were attributed to the lack of implementation in this research. These reasons give some empirical colour to the laundry list of issues delineated above. For example, when it comes to the supply side of recommendations, all these inquiries principally, and in many cases exclusively, drew their evidence through quasi-judicial proceedings. This one-dimensional approach to generating lessons had a series of negative implications. First, there were few attempts to synthesise different forms of knowledge beyond the witness box into recommendations. Neither lived experience, via the participatory function, nor policy research, via the lesson-learning function, were a common feature of these Commissions. They were essentially *monocentric* in terms of data generation and knowledge construction. Second, all the inquiries were either described as politically motivated or excessively adversarial by interviewees. For example, the Royal Commission into Trade Union Governance and Corruption (2014) was convened to lesson-learn and prompt policy change within Australia's unions. The party-political effects it produced, its combative approach to evidence-taking, its focus on criminal prosecutions and, most importantly, the fact that its recommendations tended to promote pre-existing government policy, all meant that its recommendations were not perceived as genuine attempts at programmatic reform. It therefore failed the first criterion of effectiveness set out above – the production of recommendations perceived to be valid. Finally, the over emphasis on legal-judicial logic in these Commissions meant that there was lack of policy 'craft' influencing the construction of knowledge (Stark et al. 2023). Notable here is the one inquiry in the sample that came close to resembling a policy review, as it was implemented in its entirety. This Commission, the Equine Influenza Inquiry, delivered a more review-like final report, and accompanied it with some clever bureaucratic design features, which included the establishment of an implementation monitor to report on the actioning of recommendations. This understanding of implementation challenges was one reason why its recommendations were viewed positively by those required to action them (Stark et al. 2023: 11).

These problems all point us towards the beginning of an argument about inquiry design and its connection with effectiveness. Our initial claim relates solely to the first criterion of effectiveness that was set out above, namely the development of valid recommendations. In this regard, our argument is simply that inquiry designs which include only one mode of data generation and knowledge construction have a tendency be less effective than those which rely on a plurality of methodologies. In other words, *data generation and knowledge production processes that are monocentric tend to be less effective.* When it comes to policy functions, moreover, the degree to which this is an issue seems to increase if the exclusive mode of analysis is being delivered by a legal-judicial logic.

We can develop this argument further by reflecting on our second criterion of success, which is the extent to which recommendations are implemented and the degree to which they go on to produce policy outcomes. Two explanations that account for the weak levels of implementation we often see following inquiries allow us to think about inquiry design features. The first relates to the politics of policy implementation, which often derails efforts to create change. In the case of the Australian Royal Commissions, for example, executives that were largely indifferent to certain recommendations simply reframed them in ways which rendered them benign and required minimal forms of action, or in some examples no action at all (Brown and Stark 2022). This kind of 'calculated inaction' (McConnell and 't Hart 2019) shows up in the autopsy of many inquiry recommendations and represents one of a range of tokenistic gestures that allow would-be implementers to commit to reform without ever investing in it seriously (Brown and Stark 2022).

A second and more mundane explanation relates to the characteristics of modern policy environments. This explanation tells us that in overcrowded policy arenas in which organisations face significant pressures, there is a tendency to focus exclusively on core business. Often inquiry recommendations arrive at the desks of officials in these organisations without any legislative mandate, additional resources for implementation or champion supporting them. Without these incentives they are simply swallowed up and lost in the everyday churn of public sectors because actors are simply not inclined to give up finite resources to address them (Brown and Stark 2022). Therefore, the capacity of recommendations to travel across organisational borders and find accommodation with willing hosts is a crucial factor in their effectiveness. They are hampered in this regard not just by a lack of incentives, however, but also by the fact that inquiry recommendations are not re-tailored to the organisation that receives them. Without a process of re-translation, they can arrive at a host's door without the context specificity that is required to get them accommodation and support. Sometimes they will be turned away because they demand too much in financial or practical terms and would-be implementers simply file them in the 'too hard basket'. At other times, inquiry lessons will be viewed as the products of central actors who do not understand distant jurisdictions or different levels of government.

If we return to our argument about pluralities, what we see in the discussion above is that having too many actors in a reform process actually works against effective implementation. Recommendations enter this environment, transfer around and are championed or lost because of a variety of environmental characteristics, and the pluralistic nature of this context means that ownership, responsibility, and accountability are absent. This tells us that effectiveness could be improved by locating steering and/or oversight of implementation via a single organisation. For example, if an executive is not prepared to lead on a reform agenda, independent implementation monitors can deliver oversight and policy development functions that can avoid the kind of reframing and offloading which has killed off many inquiry recommendations. Thus, at this stage of an inquiry process, *monocentric control of implementation processes is to be preferred* and the *centralisation of reform responsibility* through one or two actors with steering responsibilities should be promoted.

4.3 Understanding Inquiry Design through Success

Our arguments have emerged from examples of inquiry failure, but they can be developed further through discussions of success in which we see the opposite. If we examine inquiries which have had their recommendations well supported, for example, we often find plurality and polycentrism in the methods and rationality that are used to generate them.

We can think first about how a variety of rationalities and corresponding epistemologies within an inquiry can enhance its effectiveness. For example, the International Commission of Inquiry on East Timor used a very typical legal judicial logic for its evidence gathering that focused on war crimes and prosecution. However, the Commission was also concerned with reconciliation. It therefore used forensic anthropologists and modes of community engagement to assist its evidence taking. Although expensive and slow in terms of proceedings, these additional dimensions were said to have led to the generation of evidence from unanticipated sources, and to have contributed to post-conflict reconstruction by giving victims and communities voice. However, what is important for our discussion of design is that the use of a combination of legal-judicial, participatory and reconciliatory logics meant that the Commission's recommendations were supported. As one analysis noted at the time 'the combination of criminal prosecution, on the one hand, and community-based reconciliation procedures, on the other, reflects a sophisticated approach to addressing past human rights tragedies while meeting the practical realities of a transitional process' (Stahn 2001: 966). In another example, the Commission of Enquiry on the Practice of Untouchability against Scheduled Castes and Scheduled Tribes was headed by a single judge who was given fairly technical terms of reference reflecting a 'law and order' perspective on the eradication of untouchability. As Srinivasulu (2017) argues, this focus was likely to produce ineffective recommendations due to the social and religious entrenchment of the issue. However, commission staff extensively travelled through the Indian state of Andhra Pradesh to build links with community leaders and caste and professional associations. This enabled the collection of material of such 'depth and quantum' that it enabled the Commission to go beyond the technical terms of reference and extend the framing of untouchability to a larger social problem to be solved by mass mobilisation of communities and civil society groups (Srinivasulu 2017).

Pluralism can also relate to the use of a variety methods. Good researchers know that triangulation is important because the validity of data and the inferences drawn from it grow stronger when common themes emerge across multiple methods. The same is true for inquiries. In this sense, multiple methods can be used within a single professional logic. For example, typical cross-examination and questioning via lawyer can be complemented by other means, such as the use of private witness statements, which were used successfully in the Commission of Inquiry into the Collision of Vessels near Lamma Island in Hong Kong and the Royal Commission into Institutional Child Sexual Abuse in Australia. Inquiries can also use a variety of different styles of questioning, such as the 'hot tub' method used in the Victorian Royal Commission into Family Violence. This method uses panels of witnesses simultaneously as a means of creating knowledge in a co-constitutive manner (see Rares 2013). Modes of policy analysis and the use of expert panels are common in many inquiries, but other inquiries have innovated in this area with some degrees of success. The Canterbury Earthquakes Royal Commission, for example, deployed a peer review process which invited specific papers on building collapses from the government, then sent these out to international experts for review. This enhanced the extent to which the Commission was able to understand the reasons why an earthquake that was low in magnitude managed to cause such extensive damage (Stark 2018).

Finally, there is also a connection between effectiveness and polycentricism in terms of the actors involved in an inquiry episode. We can think about actors in a narrow sense in terms of the actors involved in an inquiry. For example, there are many examples of successful inquiries which have had multiple chairs or commissioners. There are a number of advantages to be had in this regard. Many chairs can dilute the adversarial nature that can creep into an inquiry when led by a judge (Timmins 2019). They can also bring much needed expertise or 'savvy' into proceedings through an understanding of the real world of policy or politics, increasing the practicality of the recommendations (Meyer et al. 2020). In addition, multiple chairs can mean that reports speak to multiple audiences, which is important if implementation requires an array of organisations. The Royal Commission into the Pike River Coal Mine Tragedy in New Zealand, for example, utilised a mining commissioner from Australia alongside the former chief executive of the Electoral Commission, who had significant experience of public service. Both sat alongside a judge in a three-person panel. This is a potent combination as the authority of the judge and the knowledge of the expert can be facilitated by the ability of a co-chair who understands how policy is created and implemented (and how recommendations might be shelved). Another way of addressing the 'implementability' issue also involves increasing the plurality of actors: as Timmins (2019) notes, there can be utility in testing the practicality of recommendations with policymakers and practitioners before they are finalised. Similarly, we can think about the plurality of actors involved in gaining support for an inquiry's work. According to Mintrom et al. (2021), engaging with advocacy coalitions (pre-existing networks of people who share values and act in a coordinated manner) was a feature of three inquiries that all had significant policy influence.

More broadly, an innovative way of thinking about inquiries is to view them as one element of a larger lesson-learning endeavour. In this regard, an individual inquiry can be viewed as one actor in a constellation of efforts that are all calibrated towards learning. These constellations often materialise in the wake of serious crises as many organisations seek for their own specific learnings. The most obvious example of this in recent times can be seen in the sheer volume of lessons that are emerging about COVID-19, which are institutionally fragmented and driven by a range of logics. In such contexts, one way of designing effectiveness into a process of inquiry learning is to coordinate across different inquiries that convened at the same time by different sponsors (Meyer et al. 2020). This kind of coordination has happened before, albeit informally, after the SARS outbreak of 2003–4 in Ontario. In response to this outbreak, three inquiries were convened: 1) The Ontario Expert Panel on SARS and Infectious Disease Control, which was primarily oriented towards public health, medical and scientific practitioners at a provincial level; 2) The SARS Commission, which still focused on public health policy, but also addressed the thornier issue of holding political decision-makers to account, as well as tougher policy questions around, for example, local government restructuring; 3) a review by the National Advisory Committee on SARS, which focused on public health dimensions at the national level. Each of these mechanisms had a different focus and was structured differently. The first delivered lessons for frontline medical practitioners, the second focused on policy, politics and government broadly and the third provided evidence-based analysis at the national. However, the crucial point is that each chair was in communication with the others in the early stages of inquiry design, during their proceedings, and once their reports were released. This coordination facilitated a proper division of labour and expertise and led to final reports that also supported a range of common positions with different evidence. The result was an inter-connected learning episode which encouraged a significant amount of policy change (Stark 2018). With these kinds of insights in mind, Meyer et al. (2020) recommended a two-stage COVID-19 inquiry process for the United Kingdom – first a lesson-learning inquiry led by knowledge brokers, and second a statutory inquiry focused on fact-finding, accountability and restoring public trust.

The SARS example tells us once again that when it comes to the design of inquiries, effectiveness can be created by introducing *polycentricism into the processes that produce knowledge*. However, when it comes to the other side of the effectiveness coin, the extent of implementation, studies that offer a chance to analyse success are rare. This is in part because inquiry literature rarely examines implementation specifically, preferring instead to measure broad outcomes rather than the specific processes that produced them (Stark et al. 2023). Nevertheless, we have enough to reinforce our argument. For example, many of the inquiries which were discussed above in relation to lesson-learning after crises have had good implementation rates and some have been implemented in their entirety. In those cases, the severity of the focusing events and the tragedies around them ensured that executives owned the responsibility for implementation. This is the ideal scenario as it means that a single, authoritative body takes charge of championing the reform agenda.

However, the successful royal commissions analysed by Mintrom et al. (2021) were all implemented wholly or in part by governments other than those who commissioned them. A common thread in those cases was that they engaged in narrative framing to ensure their findings and recommendations would transcend partisan politics. Importantly, they also paid significant attention not only to crafting implementable recommendations, but specifically guiding or monitoring implementation. One mechanism is to recommend the creation of specific agencies that will lead on the implementation of an inquiry's recommendations. In the case of the SARS crisis discussed above, for example, Public Health Ontario was created as a consequence of the inquiry lesson learning which took place. It would go on to champion the letter and the spirit of the inquiries that led to its creation. While not as authoritative as an executive, these champions still own and encourage the implementation process. Moreover, they hold the institutional memory of the lesson-learning that led to their creation, which is important if reform efforts exist over the longer-term (Stark and Head 2019). Another option is for inquiries to reconvene after a period of time to monitor implementation progress themselves, as was the case with the Bichard inquiry into the Soham murders (Timmins 2019). A final means of establishing oversight and ownership of recommendations is the implementation monitor. These offices, which are independently created and designed to publicise implementation progress around recommendations, often encourage implementers to accept responsibility, as in the case of the Equine Influenza Inquiry (which was fully implemented). They may also take on responsibilities for policy development themselves, as in the Victorian Bushfires Royal Commission (also fully implemented). In both cases, implementation was enhanced because the monitor role encouraged greater degrees of ownership of the implementation process.

These examples once again help us develop our argument about effectiveness because they show that *centralising authority for implementation is a means of controlling the complexity of a reform process*. It is this complexity that breeds inaction, either as an environmental factor in which recommendations are lost, or as strategic factor which implementers use to 'lose' recommendations. This is not to say that many different actors are not required to implement an inquiry's wishes. The implementation space will always be a context of plurality just because of the fragmented and differentiated nature of modern governance. However, when a single actor owns the reform agenda, hostile environments are less likely to kill off recommendations before they are implemented.

These two design arguments, at a theoretical level, can be expressed simply in a classic 2×2 scheme (Table 1) in which the location of the design variables and their polycentric character are both emphasised in relation to our two effectiveness criteria (quality of lessons and degree of implementation).

It is certainly instructive to get to the heart of the theoretical issues when it comes to design and to distil them in this way. However, what are the practical design features which can ensure that an inquiry is polycentric in its knowledge creation and monocentric at the implementation stage? We can offer several of our own recommendations in this area. In terms of bringing in multiple logics to the internal constitution of an inquiry, designers ought to think about:

• **Multiple chairs with different skillsets and professional histories**. If a senior or retired judge is required because of, for example, statutory frameworks which delineate certain inquiry design features, they can always be assisted by additional chairs. Thought should be given in this regard to those who may have experience of the policy area in question but also broader forms of experience that may be germane to the process of lesson-learning and policy implementation.
• **Multiple forms of evidence gathering.** If a plurality of data is sought through an inquiry, then a plurality of different methods will be required.

Table 1 The essence of effective inquiry design

	Monocentric design	**Polycentric design**
Internal inquiry constitution (Rationality/Methods/Actors)	Ineffective lesson learning	Effective lesson learning
External inquiry environment (Fragmentation and complexity of implementation context)	Effective implementation	Ineffective implementation

This may mean going beyond the quasi courtroom setting and the more typical forms of rapporteur support in order to produce participatory mechanisms that co-constitute knowledge with a variety of communities and stakeholders. Not only does this enhance the knowledge base of an inquiry but multiple forms of evidence gathering can act as a defusing element which softens the problems caused by adversarial proceedings. One technique for encouraging wide participation is to provide funding to community groups to facilitate engagement from non-standard actors.

- **Multiple venues beyond 'the centre'.** Other than resource implications, there is nothing to stop inquiries getting away from central locations in order to engage different communities and stakeholders. Typically, senior inquiry personnel might visit specific sites and connect with individuals and groups. This is not the same as *sitting* and generating evidence in a different location, as the latter ensures less tokenism and more participatory dynamics, as was the case with the Canadian Royal Commission on the Status of Women (Grace 2014).

- **Multiple knowledge brokers and knowledge synthesisers.** As we discussed above in relation to the lesson learning function, multiple actors can mean conflict over the methods used and outcomes sought in an inquiry. In order to manage this, inquiries need personnel who can act as brokers and synthesisers. Brokers help deliver forms of knowledge that span across boundaries (Haas 2015), and these often take the shape of specific advisory panels with a mix of expertise and synthesisers in the form of individuals who have experience with a variety of epistemologies, methods and professions. These individuals can be indispensable when it comes to coordinating and cohering knowledge creation efforts with inquiries.

Although an inquiry is not responsible for the task of implementing its own lessons, there are still several things which can be recommended that have the potential to centralise and cohere the implementation effort. The first and most important step, however, is for those within inquiries to accept that designing for implementation is part of their task. Sticking to a separation of tasks in which an inquiry generates knowledge and leaves all thought of implementation to an executive is guaranteed route to inaction. More specifically:

- **Co-constituting design features with stakeholders.** When stakeholders are included in the design and running of an inquiry, they will be more inclined to champion its lessons and implement its recommendations. Including stakeholders in design decisions, as the Grenfell Tower Inquiry did in relation to its terms of reference for example, can be a means of generating legitimacy. Centralisation and reform momentum can be created through this legitimacy and the champions it creates. Testing recommendations with practitioners and other stakeholders before finalising the report is another co-creation method.

- **Using independent implementation monitors.** Monitors that report directly to parliaments and broadcast progress in terms of delivery are an effective means of generating coherence and incentivising action around recommendations. Typically, when monitors are used implementation rates increase (see Stark 2018; Brown and Stark 2022).

- **Recognition of transfer and translation requirements.** When designing and drafting recommendations inquiries need to recognise the need to be persuasive so that their knowledge has the capacity to travel across different organisations. This means recognising the organisational landscape of implementation, the challenges that implementing organisations face and it also means supporting them when it comes to effecting change. At the narrow end, inquiries may simply design knowledge that is outcome focused rather than prescriptive, which can allow implementers room for manoeuvre. At a larger scale, supporting recommendations might be made that support implementers in terms of finance, personnel or implementation routes.

- **Post-publication communications.** If inquiry chairs and senior personnel are fully independent, there is nothing to stop them from advocating on behalf of their recommendations once they have published their report(s) and the inquiry has shut up shop. Centralising coherence can be achieved by clever communication strategies as the 9/11 Commissioners showed. Moreover, having active personnel post-publication can be a means of translating and communicating recommendations across different contexts, thus ensuring that knowledge transfer takes place. For example, the US Maine Wabanaki-State Child Welfare Truth and Reconciliation Commission partnered with a community working group that continued advocating for the work of the Commission beyond the end of its mandate (Centala 2016).

4.4 Bringing in Policy Tools Knowledge to Inquiry Design

While the discussion above draws on the inquiry literature, we can also learn lessons from the policy design scholarship. There should be no question that when it comes to policy design, the largest contribution that has been made is in relation to our understanding of the 'policy mix' (Flanagan et al. 2011). Indeed, when asking what, if anything, is known with certainty in this field, the answer is likely to be that we know much more about the nature of a variety of policy tools, the distinctions that separate them, and how they can be brought together into effective configurations (Capano and Howlett 2020: 3). Thus, amongst other things, policy design literature helps us to distinguish between procedural and substantive policy tools (Jordan and Turnpenny 2015), between tools used for 'packaging' new reforms and tools needed to 'patch up' existing policies (Howlett and Mukherjee 2014), and between tools that can be used within certain types of governance architecture but not others (Capano et al. 2015). This knowledge could be harnessed by those who propose recommendations to ensure that what is being proposed has the capacity to deliver what is intended. Reflections of this nature have appeared in successful inquiries. The Pitt Inquiry in the United Kingdom, for example, spent some considerable effort mapping out implementation routes, costing recommendations and analysing the compatibility of the policy tools it recommended with the capacities of the agencies that had to action them. This was recognised as one reason why it was extensively implemented (Stark 2018). Efforts of this nature would certainly be enhanced via a greater synthesis of lesson-learning, report writing and policy tools thinking. However, perhaps most importantly, this research also gives us an understanding of how different actors lend support to different types of policy tool (Voß and Simons 2014; Béland and Howlett 2016). Works of this nature could also influence inquiry decisions, particularly when implementation is likely to be fraught.

Central to all these works is an assumption that getting the policy mix correct at the design stage will mean greater coherence when it comes implementation. While it is certainly possible to reflect on this assumption critically, largely because of the chaotic dynamics of the policy world (see Flanagan et al. 2011), the sheer volume of attention given to analysing policy mixes does suggest that they ought to be considered as another design feature for the public inquiry. This view is supported by the fact that design scholars themselves tell us that effectiveness is influenced by a capacity to get the mix of tools right (Peters et al. 2018: 16–17). This takes us to a third dimension of our argument about plurality which is that *inquiry recommendations ought to be developed in ways which give consideration to the mix of policy tools and their complementarity*. It is likely that a mix – or plurality – of tools will be required and those who design recommendations need to consider them as a package that will affect coherence and incoherence at the delivery stage. Evidence does exist that shows the negative effects which can emerge if inquiries do not think about the complementarity of the recommendations they propose. One outcome, for example, is the need for policy refinement via subsequent policy analysis mechanisms that are created after an inquiry. These mechanisms are often required to arbitrate between recommendations and outcomes proposed by inquiries which sit in tension with each other. After the Victorian Bushfires Royal Commission in Australia, for example, a taskforce had to be convened to reconcile the need for safe energy infrastructure with the need for more community and expert involvement in risk management decision-making (Stark 2018). More consideration of how these goals might sit in tension as a policy mix may have prevented the need for further policy analysis, debate and (eventually) the modification of that inquiry's infrastructure recommendations.

This argument adds a final element into our design thinking. If we consider a polycentric design to be one in which recommendations represent a properly considered policy mix of tools, they would have at least three features. First, they would use a mix of procedural and substantive instruments with a deliberate focus on the role of each. Second, they would clearly identify which tools are for packaging new policy and which are for patching existing policy. Finally, recommendations would be presented with analyses of the governance architecture that they would sit within most effectively. With this final addition in mind, we can now return to our table of inquiry effectiveness.

Table 2 encapsulates our three dimensional argument about the fundamentals of inquiry design, which we have argued is a form of policy design very relevant to inquiry effectiveness. These elements ought to be considered both by those in government designing inquiries (e.g., through the selection of members and the terms of reference) and inquiry members and staff designing inquiry structures and processes from the inside. At the centre of the argument developed above is a claim that plurality is a key variable influencing effectiveness in the three dimensions of internal inquiry constitution, policy tool selection and external inquiry environment (i.e., implementation context). By effectiveness, we mean the degree to which recommendations are capable of addressing the issues that the inquiry was convened to address, and the extent to which those recommendations are implemented to good effect (again in relation to the issues that the inquiry was to address). Building on this view of effectiveness, we argue that

Table 2 Monocentric v polycentric designs and inquiry effectiveness

	Monocentric design	**Polycentric design**
Internal inquiry constitution (Rationality/methods/actors)	Ineffective lesson learning	Effective lesson learning
Policy tool selection (Range of policy mix and complementarity within)	Ineffective outcomes	Effective outcomes
External inquiry environment (Fragmentation and complexity of implementation context)	Effective implementation	Ineffective implementation

inquiries which are polycentric in terms of knowledge construction and policy tool/recommendation selection are likely to produce outputs which have the capacity to be effective. However, when it comes to implementation, our argument is the opposite, namely that monocentric implementation processes, which reduce complexity through the centralisation of responsibility in a limited number of actors, are more likely to lead to inquiry success.

5 Conclusion

In this Element, we have attempted to achieve three objectives. The first was to show how the practices performed by policy designers are not so different from those performed by those who operate within public inquiries. While each type of actor operates in a very different context, making comparisons between the two interesting, both are primarily concerned with conducting policy analyses and recommending advice to decision-makers in the form of changed policy programmes and tools. This means that at a fundamental level the scholarship around policy design and that concerned with public inquiries do not represent 'worlds apart'. We have sought to bring those two worlds closer together here by conceptualising the inquiry as a procedural policy tool and showing that it can also be an important policy design space and a producer of important design functions. Conversely, we argued that design scholarship can help us better conceptualise the complex processes that constitute inquiry learning, knowledge production and advice giving, and can assist with resolving the incoherence and fragmentation currently characterising inquiry literature. These two worlds of scholarship have something to offer each other, and both sets of scholars can benefit from making more connections between them.

Our second objective was to use a range of international examples to highlight the inquiry functions that are most relevant to policy design. This has led us to propose four design functions as especially important, both in terms of the regularity with which they are produced and their potential effectiveness in the future. These are the catalytic function; the learning function; the processual function and the legitimation function. Through the elucidation of these four functions, we have sought to show the relevance of the inquiry to policy design, but we also hope that the international nature of our examples is not lost on the reader. In this regard our examples certainly are 'worlds apart' as they come from Asia, Africa, Europe, North America and Australasia and they cover a full range of different policy concerns. They have been gathered here deliberately to show a glimpse of the many and varied ways in which inquiries operate around the world. What connects them all, however, are our four policy design functions. Regardless of context, these functions stand up as *the* primary means through which public inquiries show their continued relevance to public policy. In the future, when someone asks what use public inquiries are in relation to public policy, these four functions ought to represent a clear and unequivocal answer. Public inquiries can propel policy change, they can deliver analyses and lessons about policy, they can help design the processes that action it and they can produce forms of participation that help support and legitimise it.

Our final objective was to consider the policy design choices inherent in designing inquiries for effectiveness. We proposed our own recommendations about how to design for effectiveness, and particularly to maximise inquiries' policy design potential. Underneath the specifics, we proposed that plurality should be a key concern when it comes to designing and using a public inquiry. It is helpful to build in plurality to the internal mechanics of an inquiry because, we argue, successful inquiries tend to be those that use a range of methods to construct their knowledge. Plurality is also an important consideration when it comes to formulating recommendations because, as design literature shows consistently, effectiveness often requires a mix of multiple policy tools of different types. However, we have argued that when it comes to the implementation of inquiry recommendations 'less is more' because recommendations tend to get lost in the complex constellations of actors that are required to action inquiries. At this stage, centralisation and monocentricity ought to be prioritised above plurality so that inquiries do not end up gathering dust on a forgotten shelf.

References

Abele, F. (2014). The Lasting Impact of the Berger Inquiry into the Construction of a Pipeline in the Mackenzie Valley. In G. J. Inwood & C. M. Johns, (Eds.), *Commissions of Inquiry and Policy Change: A Comparative Analysis* (pp. 88–112). University of Toronto Press.

Access to Biological Resources in Commonwealth Areas Inquiry. (2000). Access to Biological Resources in Commonwealth Areas. https://library .dbca.wa.gov.au/static/FullTextFiles/926054.pdf.

Acland, H. (1980). Research as Stage Management: The Case of the Plowdon Committee. In M. Bulmer, (Ed.), *Social Research and Royal Commissions* (pp. 19–34). George Allen & Unwin.

Althaus, C. (1994). Legitimation and Agenda Setting: Development and the Environment in Australia and Canada's North. In P. Weller, (Ed.),*Royal Commissions and the Making of Public Policy* (pp. 186–97). Centre for Australian Public Sector Management.

Ashforth, A. (1990). Reckoning Schemes of Legitimation: On Commissions of Inquiry as Power/Knowledge Forms. *Journal of Historical Sociology, 3*(1), 1–22. https://doi.org/10.1111/j.1467-6443.1990.tb00143.x.

Bali, A. S., Capano, G., & Ramesh, M. (2019). Anticipating and Designing for Policy Effectiveness. *Policy and Society, 38*(1), 1–13. https://doi.org/ 10.1080/14494035.2019.1579502.

Bali, A. S., Howlett, M., Lewis, J. M., & Ramesh, M. (2021). Procedural Policy Tools in Theory and Practice. *Policy and Society, 40*(3), 295–311. https://doi .org/10.1080/14494035.2021.1965379.

Bauer, M. W., Green-Pedersen, C., Héritier, A., & Jordan, A. (2012). *Dismantling Public Policy: Preferences, Strategies, and Effects.* Oxford University Press.

Beer, J. (2011). *Public Inquiries.* Oxford University Press.

Béland, D., & Howlett, M. (2016). How Solutions Chase Problems: Instrument Constituencies in the Policy Process. *Governance, 29*(3), 393–409. https:// doi.org/10.1111/gove.12179.

Blomkamp, E. (2022). Systemic Design Practice for Participatory Policymaking. *Policy Design and Practice, 5*(1), 12–31. https://doi.org/ 10.1080/25741292.2021.1887576.

Boin, A., 't Hart, P., Stern, E., & Sundelius, B. (2016). *The Politics of Crisis Management: Understanding Public Leadership When It Matters Most.* 2nd ed. Cambridge University Press.

Boudes, T., & Laroche, H. (2009). Taking Off the Heat: Narrative Sensemaking in Post-crisis Inquiry Reports. *Organization Studies, 30*(4), 377–96. https://doi.org/10.1177/0170840608101141.

Bovens, M. A. P., 't Hart, P., & Peters, B. G. (2001). *Success and Failure in Public Governance: A Comparative Analysis.* Edward Elgar.

Brown, A. D. (2000). Making Sense of Inquiry Sensemaking. *Journal of Management Studies, 37*(1), 45–75. https://doi.org/10.1111/1467-6486.00172.

Brown, A. D. (2004). Authoritative Sensemaking in a Public Inquiry Report. *Organization Studies, 25*(1), 95–112. https://doi.org/10.1177/0170840604038182.

Brown, P. R., & Stark, A. (2022). Policy Inaction Meets Policy Learning: Four Moments of Non-implementation. *Policy Sciences, 55*(1), 47–63. https://doi.org/10.1007/s11077-021-09446-y.

Buckley, H., & O'Nolan, C. (2013). *An Examination of Recommendations from Inquiries into Events in Families and Their Interactions with State Services, and Their Impact on Policy and Practice.* Department of Children and Youth Affairs. www.lenus.ie/handle/10147/315231.

Buckmaster, L., & Clark, S. (2018). *The National Disability Insurance Scheme: A Chronology* (Research Paper Series, 2018–19). Parliamentary Library. www.aph.gov.au/About_Parliament/Parliamentary_Departments/Parliamentary_Library/pubs/rp/rp1819/Chronologies/NDIS.

Bulmer, M. (Ed.). (1980). *Social Research and Royal Commissions.* George Allen & Unwin.

Capano, G., & Howlett, M. (2020). The Knowns and Unknowns of Policy Instrument Analysis: Policy Tools and the Current Research Agenda on Policy Mixes. *SAGE Open, 10*(1). https://doi.org/10.1177/2158244019900568.

Capano, G., & Howlett, M. (2022). How Tools Work: Policy Instruments as Activators and Mechanisms. In M. Howlett, (Ed.), *The Routledge Handbook of Policy Tools* (1st ed., pp. 61–72). Routledge. https://doi.org/10.4324/9781003163954.

Capano, G., Howlett, M., & Ramesh, M. (Eds.). (2015). *Varieties of Governance: Dynamics, Strategies, Capacities.* Springer.

Carey, G., Dickinson, H., Malbon, E., & Reeders, D. (2018). The Vexed Question of Market Stewardship in the Public Sector: Examining Equity and the Social Contract through the Australian National Disability Insurance Scheme. *Social Policy & Administration, 52*(1), 387–407. https://doi.org/10.1111/spol.12321.

Carter, N. (1989). Performance Indicators: 'Backseat Driving' or 'Hands Off' Control? *Policy & Politics, 17*(2), 131–8. https://doi.org/10.1332/030557389782454857.

Centala, E. P. (2016). *Redefining Transitional Justice in the North American Context? The Maine Wabanaki-State Child Welfare Truth and Reconciliation Commission* [Master of Arts]. University of Maine.

Chapman, R. A. (1973). Commissions in Policy-Making. In R. A. Chapman, (Ed.), *The Role of Commissions in Policy-Making* (pp. 174–88). George Allen & Unwin.

Christensen, J., & Holst, C. (2017). Advisory Commissions, Academic Expertise and Democratic Legitimacy: The Case of Norway. *Science and Public Policy, 44*(6), 821–33. https://doi.org/10.1093/scipol/scx016.

Clokie, H. D., & Robinson, W. J. (1937). *Royal Commissions of Inquiry.* Stanford University Press.

Commonwealth of Australia. (2019). Commonwealth Letters Patent Amended 13 September 2019. https://disability.royalcommission.gov.au/system/files/2021-11/Commonwealth%20Letters%20Patent%20amended%2013%20September%202019.pdf.

Compton, M., & 't Hart, P. (Eds.). (2019). *Great Policy Successes.* Oxford University Press.

Cunneen, C. (2001). Assessing the Outcomes of the Royal Commission into Aboriginal Deaths in Custody. *Health Sociology Review, 10*(2), 53–64. https://doi.org/10.5172/hesr.2001.10.2.53.

De Smedt, P., & Borch, K. (2022). Participatory Policy Design in System Innovation. *Policy Design and Practice, 5*(1), 51–65. https://doi.org/10.1080/25741292.2021.1887592.

deLeon, P. (1978). Public Policy Termination: An End and a Beginning. *Policy Analysis, 4*(3), 369–92.

Donson, F., & O'Donovan, D. (2022). Public Inquiries and Administrative Justice. In M. Hertogh, R. Kirkham, R. Thomas, & J. Tomlinson, (Eds.), *The Oxford Handbook of Administrative Justice* (pp. 137–54). Oxford University Press. https://doi.org/10.1093/oxfordhb/9780190903084.013.9.

Douglas, S., Schillemans, T., 't Hart, P. et al. (2021). Rising to Ostrom's Challenge: An Invitation to Walk on the Bright Side of Public Governance and Public Service. *Policy Design and Practice, 4*(4), 441–51. https://doi.org/10.1080/25741292.2021.1972517.

Dunlop, C., & Radaelli, C. M. (2021). The Lessons of Policy Learning: Types, Triggers, Hindrances and Pathologies. In C. Weible & P. Cairney, (Eds.), *Practical Lessons from Policy Theories* (pp. 83–104). Bristol: Policy Press.

Dunlop, C. A., & Radaelli, C. M. (2013). Systematising Policy Learning: From Monolith to Dimensions. *Political Studies*, *61*(3), 599–619. https://doi.org/10.1111/j.1467-9248.2012.00982.x.

Dwyer, G. (2021). Learning to Learn from Bushfire: Perspectives from Victorian Emergency Management Practitioners. *Australian Journal of Public Administration*, *80*(3), 602–12. https://doi.org/10.1111/1467-8500.12476.

Eburn, M., & Dovers, S. (2015). Learning Lessons from Disasters: Alternatives to Royal Commissions and Other Quasi-Judicial Inquiries. *Australian Journal of Public Administration*, *74*(4), 495–508. https://doi.org/10.1111/1467-8500.12115.

Elliott, D. (2009). The Failure of Organizational Learning from Crisis – A Matter of Life and Death? *Journal of Contingencies and Crisis Management*, *17*(3), 157–68. https://doi.org/10.1111/j.1468-5973.2009.00576.x.

Elliott, D., & McGuinness, M. (2002). Public Inquiry: Panacea or Placebo? *Journal of Contingencies and Crisis Management*, *10*(1), 14–25. https://doi.org/10.1111/1468-5973.00177.

Falkenrath, R. A. (2004). The 9/11 Commission Report. *International Security*, *29*(3), 170–90.

Fischer, F. (2003). *Reframing Public Policy: Discursive Politics and Deliberative Practices*. Oxford University Press.

Flanagan, K., Uyarra, E., & Laranja, M. (2011). Reconceptualising the 'Policy Mix' for Innovation. *Research Policy*, *40*(5), 702–13. https://doi.org/10.1016/j.respol.2011.02.005.

Flinders, M., Mulgan, G., & Stark, A. (2021). Range and Variety in Models of Public Inquiry: How to Stimulate Innovative Inquiry Design, Process and Practice. 12 October. IPPO. https://theippo.co.uk/range-variety-models-public-inquiry-innovative-inquiry-design-process-practice/

Gephart Jnr, R. P. (1993). The Textual Approach: Risk and Blame in Disaster Sensemaking. *Academy of Management of Journal*, *38*(6), 1465–514.

Gibbs, E. (2022). What Royal Commission? 6 March. Patreon. www.patreon.com/elgibbs/posts.

Gouache, C. (2022). Imagining the Future with Citizens: Participatory Foresight and Democratic Policy Design in Marcoussis, France. *Policy Design and Practice*, *5*(1), 66–85. https://doi.org/10.1080/25741292.2021.1930687.

Goudge, S. (2016). The Berger Inquiry in Retrospect: Its Legacy. *Canadian Journal of Women and the Law*, *28*(2), 393–407.

Grace, J. (2014). Politics and Promise: A Feminist-Institutionalist Analysis of the Royal Commission on the Status of Women. In G. J. Inwood, & C. M. Johns,

(Eds.), *Commissions of Inquiry and Policy Change: A Comparative Analysis* (pp. 70–87). University of Toronto Press.

Haas, A. (2015). Crowding at the Frontier: Boundary Spanners, Gatekeepers and Knowledge Brokers. *Journal of Knowledge Management, 19*(5), 1029–47. https://doi.org/10.1108/JKM-01-2015-0036.

Hall, P. (1993). Policy Paradigms, Social Learning and the State. *Comparative Politics, 25*(3), 275–96.

Hansen, P., Sivesind, K., & Thostrup, R. (2021). Managing Expectations by Projecting the Future School: Observing the Nordic Future School Reports via Temporal Topologies. *European Educational Research Journal, 20*(6), 860–74. https://doi.org/10.1177/1474904121995695.

Head, B. W. (2022). *Wicked Problems in Public Policy: Understanding and Responding to Complex Challenges*. Springer International. https://doi.org/10.1007/978-3-030-94580-0.

Heclo, H. (1974). *Modern Social Politics in Britain and Sweden: From Relief to Income Maintenance*. Yale University Press.

Herbert, A. (1961). Anything but Action? A Study of the Uses and Abuses of Committees of Inquiry. In R. Harris, (Ed.), *Radical Reaction: Essays in Competition and Affluence*. Hutchinson.

Herweg, N. (2016). Explaining European Agenda-Setting Using the Multiple Streams Framework: The Case of European Natural Gas Regulation. *Policy Sciences, 49*(1), 13–33. https://doi.org/10.1007/s11077-015-9231-z.

Hesstvedt, S., & Christensen, J. (2023). Political and Administrative Control of Expert Groups – A Mixed-Methods Study. *Governance, 36*(2), 337–57. https://doi.org/10.1111/gove.12599.

Hesstvedt, S., & Christiansen, P. M. (2022). The Politics of Policy Inquiry Commissions: Denmark and Norway, 1971–2017. *West European Politics, 45*(2), 430–54. https://doi.org/10.1080/01402382.2020.1858597.

Hillgren, P., Light, A., & Strange, M. (2020). Future Public Policy and Its Knowledge Base: Shaping Worldviews through Counterfactual World-Making. *Policy Design and Practice, 3*(2), 109–22. https://doi.org/10.1080/25741292.2020.1748372.

Hogwood, B. W., & Peters, B. G. (1983). *Policy Dynamics*. Wheatsheaf Books.

Hoppe, R. (2018). Heuristics for Practitioners of Policy Design: Rules-of-Thumb for Structuring Unstructured Problems. *Public Policy and Administration, 33* (4), 384–408. https://doi.org/10.1177/0952076717709338.

House of Commons. (2005). Public Administration Select Committee, Government by Inquiry, First Report of Session 2004–05 (Vol. I). HMSO.

Howlett, M. (2000). Managing the 'Hollow State': Procedural Policy Instruments and Modern Governance. *Canadian Public Administration, 43* (4), 412–31. https://doi.org/10.1111/j.1754-7121.2000.tb01152.x.

Howlett, M. (2009). Governance Modes, Policy Regimes and Operational Plans: A Multi-Level Nested Model of Policy Instrument Choice and Policy Design. *Policy Sciences, 42*(1), 73–89. https://doi.org/10.1007/s11077-009-9079-1.

Howlett, M. (2011). *Designing Public Policies: Principles and Instruments.* Routledge.

Howlett, M. (2019). Procedural Policy Tools and the Temporal Dimensions of Policy Design: Resilience, Robustness and the Sequencing of Policy Mixes. *International Review of Public Policy, 1*(1), 27–45.

Howlett, M. (2020). Challenges in Applying Design Thinking to Public Policy: Dealing with the Varieties of Policy Formulation and Their Vicissitudes. *Policy & Politics, 48*(1): 49–65.

Howlett, M. P., & Mukherjee, I. (2014). *Policy Design and Non-Design: Towards a Spectrum of Policy Formulation Types* [Lee Kuan Yew School of Public Policy Research Paper No. 14–11]. https://doi.org/10.2139/ssrn.2461087.

Howlett, M., & Mukherjee, I. (2017). Policy Design: From Tools to Patches. *Canadian Public Administration, 60*(1), 140–4. https://doi.org/10.1111/capa.12209.

Hudson, B., Hunter, D., & Peckham, S. (2019). Policy Failure and the Policy-Implementation Gap: Can Policy Support Programs Help? *Policy Design and Practice, 2*(1), 1–14. https://doi.org/10.1080/25741292.2018.1540378.

Hunter, A., & Boswell, C. (2015). Comparing the Political Functions of Independent Commissions: The Case of UK Migrant Integration Policy. *Journal of Comparative Policy Analysis: Research and Practice, 17*(1), 10–25. https://doi.org/10.1080/13876988.2014.896117.

Inwood, G. J., & Johns, C. M. (2014). Why Study Commissions of Inquiry? In G. J. Inwood, & C. M. Johns, (Eds.), *Commissions of Inquiry and Policy Change: A Comparative Analysis* (pp. 3–19). University of Toronto Press.

Inwood, G. J., & Johns, C. M. (2022). Tools for Structuring Policy Advice. In M. Howlett, (Ed.), *The Routledge Handbook of Policy Tools* (1st ed., pp. 208–19). Routledge. https://doi.org/10.4324/9781003163954-21.

Jain, M. (2020). The Rose That Grew from Concrete: The Commission of Inquiry into Policing in Khayelitsha, South Africa. In C. Heyns & T. Probert, (Eds.), *National Commissions of Inquiry in Africa: Vehicles to Pursue Accountability for Violations of the Right to Life?* (pp. 241–78). Pretoria University Law Press.

Jenkins, S. (2021). Public Inquiries Are Institutionally Corrupt, We Should Just Give the Money to Victims. *The Guardian*, 18 June. www.theguardian.com/commentisfree/2021/jun/17/public-inquiries-are-institutionally-corrupt-we-should-just-give-the-money-to-victims.

Johns, C. M., & Inwood, G. J. (2018). Commissions of Inquiry and Policy Analysis. In L. Dobuzinskis & M. Howlett, (Eds.), *Policy Analysis in Canada* (1st ed., pp. 233–54). Bristol University Press; JSTOR. https://doi.org/10.2307/j.ctt22rbkbb.16.

Jordan, A., & Turnpenny, J. (Eds.). (2015). *The Tools of Policy Formulation*. Edward Elgar.

Judicial Commission of Inquiry into allegations of State Capture [JCISC]. (2022). Corruption and Fraud in the Public Sector Including Organs of State. Report: Part 1. Vol. 1: Chapter 1 – *South African Airways and Its Associated Companies*. www.statecapture.org.za/.

Kay, A. (2006). *The Dynamics of Public Policy: Theory and Evidence*. Edward Elgar.

Kay, A. (2007). Tense Layering and Synthetic Policy Paradigms: The Politics of Health Insurance in Australia. *Australian Journal of Political Science*, *42*(4), 579–91. http://doi.org/10.1080/10361140701595775.

Kenny, K., & Ó Dochartaigh, N. (2021). Power and Politics in Public Inquiries: Bloody Sunday 1972. *Journal of Political Power*, *14*(3), 383–408. https://doi.org/10.1080/2158379X.2021.1890316.

Leveson, B. H. (2012). An Inquiry into the Culture, Practices and Ethics of the Press. House of Commons. www.gov.uk/government/publications/leveson-inquiry-report-into-the-culture-practices-and-ethics-of-the-press.

Lindblom, C. E. (1959). The Science of Muddling-through. *Public Administration Review*, *19*(2), 79–88.

Linder, S. H., & Peters, B. G. (1988). The Analysis of Design or the Design of Analysis? *Review of Policy Research*, *7*(4), 738–50. https://doi.org/10.1111/j.1541-1338.1988.tb00892.x.

Maffei, S., Leoni, F., & Villari, B. (2020). Data-Driven Anticipatory Governance. Emerging Scenarios in Data for Policy Practices. *Policy Design and Practice*, *3*(2), 123–34. https://doi.org/10.1080/25741292.2020.1763896.

Mahoney, J., & Thelen, K. (2010). A Theory of Gradual Institutional Change. In J. Mahoney & K. Thelen, (Eds.), *Explaining Institutional Change: Ambiguity, Agency, and Power* (pp. 1–38). Cambridge University Press.

March, J. G., & Olsen, J. P. (1984). The New Institutionalism: Organizational Factors in Political Life. *The American Political Science Review*, *78*(3), 734–49. https://doi.org/10.2307/1961840.

Marier, P. (2017). Public Inquiries. In M. Brans, I. Geva-May, & M. Howlett, (Eds.), *Routledge Handbook of Comparative Policy Analysis* (pp. 169–80). Routledge.

May, E. R. (2005). When Government Writes History. *The New Republic*. https://newrepublic.com/article/64332/when-government-writes-history.

May, P. J. (1992). Policy Learning and Failure. *Journal of Public Policy*, *12*(4), 331–54. https://doi.org/10.1017/S0143814X00005602.

May, P. J. (1991). Reconsidering Policy Design: Policies and Publics. *Journal of Public Policy*, *11*(2), 187–206. https://doi.org/10.1017/S0143814X 0000619X.

McAlinden, A.-M., & Naylor, B. (2016). Reframing Public Inquiries as 'Procedural Justice' for Victims of Institutional Child Abuse: Towards a Hybrid Model of Justice. *Sydney Law Review*, *38*(3), 277–308.

McConnell, A. (2010). Policy Success, Policy Failure and Grey Areas In-Between. *Journal of Public Policy*, *30*(3), 345–62. https://doi.org/ 10.1017/S0143814X10000152.

McConnell, A., & 't Hart, P. (2019). Inaction and Public Policy: Understanding Why Policymakers 'Do Nothing'. *Policy Sciences*, *52*(4), 645–61. https:// doi.org/10.1007/s11077-019-09362-2.

McConnell, A. (2020). The Use of Placebo Policies to Escape from Policy Traps. *Journal of European Public Policy*, *27*(7), 957–76.

Meyer, C., Ikani, N., Avendano Pabon, M., & Kelly, A. (2020). *Learning the Right Lessons for the Next Pandemic: How to Design Public Inquiries into the UK Government's Handling of COVID-19*. King's College London. https://doi.org/10.18742/PUB01-032.

Ministry of Education and Culture. (2015). *Basic Education of the Future – Let's Turn the Trend!* 12 March. https://valtioneuvosto.fi/en/-/1410845/basic-education-of-the-future-let-s-turn-the-trend-.

Mintrom, M., & Luetjens, J. (2017). Creating Public Value: Tightening Connections between Policy Design and Public Management. *Policy Studies Journal*, *45*(1), 170–90. https://doi.org/10.1111/psj.12116.

Mintrom, M., O'Neill, D., & O'Connor, R. (2021). Royal Commissions and Policy Influence. *Australian Journal of Public Administration*, *80*(1), 80–96. https://doi.org/10.1111/1467-8500.12441.

Mitchell, I., Jones, P. W., Jones, S., & Ireton, E. (2020). *The Practical Guide to Public Inquiries*. Bloomsbury Academic.

Mukherjee, I., Coban, M. K., & Bali, A. S. (2021). Policy Capacities and Effective Policy Design: A Review. *Policy Sciences*, *54*(2), 243–68. https:// doi.org/10.1007/s11077-021-09420-8.

Mulgan, G., Flinders, M., & Stark, A., (2021). *Range and Variety in Models of Public Inquiry: How to Stimulate Innovative Inquiry Design, Process and Practice*. International Public Policy Observatory. https://theippo.co.uk/range-variety-models-public-inquiry-innovative-inquiry-design-process-practice/.

Needham, C., & Dickinson, H. (2018). 'Any One of Us Could Be among That Number': Comparing the Policy Narratives for Individualized Disability Funding in Australia and England. *Social Policy & Administration, 52*(3), 731–49. https://doi.org/10.1111/spol.12320.

Parker, C. F., & Dekker, S. (2008). September 11 and Postcrisis Investigation: Exploring the Role and Impact of the 9/11 Commission. In A. Boin, A. McConnell, & P. 't Hart, (Eds.), *Governing after Crisis: The Politics of Investigation, Accountability and Learning* (pp. 255–82). Cambridge University Press

Peters, B. G., Capano, G., Howlett, M. et al. (2018). Designing for Policy Effectiveness: Defining and Understanding a Concept. Cambridge University Press. https://doi.org/10.1017/9781108555081.

Pierson, P. (2000). Increasing Returns, Path Dependence, and the Study of Politics. *American Political Science Review, 94*(2), 251–67. https://doi.org/10.2307/2586011.

Pollitt, C. (2009). Bureaucracies Remember, Post-bureaucratic Organizations Forget? *Public Administration, 87*(2), 198–218.

Posner, R. A. (2005). *Preventing Surprise Attacks: Intelligence Reform in the Wake of 9/11*. Rowman & Littlefield.

Prasser, S. (1994). Royal Commissions and Public Inquiries: Scope and Uses. In P. Weller, (Ed.), *Royal Commissions and the Making of Public Policy* (pp. 1–21). Macmillan Education.

Prasser, S. (Ed.). (2023). *New Directions in Royal Commissions and Public Inquiries: Do We Need Them?* Connor Court.

Rares, J. (2013). *Using the 'Hot Tub' – How Concurrent Expert Evidence Aids Understanding Issues* [Presentation]. 12 October. www.fedcourt.gov.au/digital-law-library/judges-speeches/justice-rares/rares-j-20131012.

Ratushny, E. (2009). *The Conduct of Public Inquiries: Law, Policy, and Practice*. Irwin Law.

Renå, H., & Christensen, J. (2020). Learning from Crisis: The Role of Enquiry Commissions. *Journal of Contingencies and Crisis Management, 28*(1), 41–9. https://doi.org/10.1111/1468-5973.12269.

Resodihardjo, S. L. (2006). Wielding a Double-Edged Sword: The Use of Inquiries at Times of Crisis. *Journal of Contingencies and Crisis Management, 14*(4), 199–206. https://doi.org/10.1111/j.1468-5973.2006.00496.x.

Resodihardjo, S. L. (2020). Inquiries Following Crises. In S. L. Resodihardjo, (Ed.), *Crises, Inquiries and the Politics of Blame* (pp. 33–45). Springer International. https://doi.org/10.1007/978-3-030-17531-3_3.

Rose, R. (1991). What Is Lesson-Drawing?. *Journal of Public Policy*, *11*(1), 3–30.

Rough, E. (2011). Policy Learning through Public Inquiries? The Case of UK Nuclear Energy Policy 1955–61. *Environment and Planning C: Government and Policy*, *29*(1), 24–45. https://doi.org/10.1068/c09184.

Roy, E. A. (2020). Christchurch Attacks: Royal Commission Hands in Report on New Zealand Mosque Shootings. *The Guardian*. 26 November. www.theguardian.com/world/2020/nov/26/christchurch-attacks-royal-commission-hands-in-report-on-new-zealand-mosque-shootings.

Saguin, K., & Cashore, B. (2022). Two Logics of Participation in Policy Design. *Policy Design and Practice*, *5*(1), 1–11. https://doi.org/10.1080/25741292.2022.2038978.

Salamon, L. (2001). The New Governance and the Tools of Public Action: An Introduction. *The Fordham Urban Law Journal*, *28*(5), 1611–74.

Salter, L. (2007). The Public of Public Inquiries. In L. Dobuzinskis, M. Howlett, & D. Laycock, (Eds.), *Policy Analysis in Canada* (pp. 289–314). University of Toronto Press. https://doi.org/10.3138/9781442685529-014.

Sanderson, I. (2002). Evaluation, Policy Learning and Evidence-Based Policy Making. *Public Administration*, *80*(1), 1–22. https://doi.org/10.1111/1467-9299.00292.

Scala, F. (2014). The Framing of Scientific Governance in Canada: Policy Change and the Royal Commission on New Reproductive Technologies. In G. J. Inwood & C. M. Johns, (Eds.), *Commissions of Inquiry and Policy Change: A Comparative Analysis* (pp. 130–53). University of Toronto Press.

Schneider, A., & Ingram, H. (1988). Systematically Pinching Ideas: A Comparative Approach to Policy Design. *Journal of Public Policy*, *8*(1), 61–80. https://doi.org/10.1017/S0143814X00006851.

Schneider, A., & Ingram, H. (1993). Social Construction of Target Populations: Implications for Politics and Policy. *American Political Science Review*, *87*(2), 334–47. https://doi.org/10.2307/2939044.

Schwartz, B. (1997). Public Inquiries. *Canadian Public Administration*, *40*(1), 72–85. https://doi.org/10.1111/j.1754-7121.1997.tb01497.x.

Snape, J. (2021). What the Split between Royal Commissioners Means for the Future of Aged Care. *ABC News*. 1 March. www.abc.net.au/news/2021-03-01/aged-care-royal-commission-division-split/13203698.

Srinivasulu, K. (2017). A Reform-Centric Approach to Ending Caste Discrimination: An Analysis of the Report of Justice Punnaiah Commission. *Review of Development and Change*, *22*(2), 109–25. https://doi.org/10.1177/0972266120170206.

Stahn, C. (2001). Accommodating Individual Criminal Responsibility and National Reconciliation: The UN Truth Commission for East Timor. *American Journal of International Law*, *95*(4), 952–66. https://doi.org/10.2307/2674655.

Stanton, K. (2022). *Reconciling Truths: Reimagining Public Inquiries in Canada*. UBC Press.

Stark, A. (2018). *Public Inquiries, Policy Learning and the Threat of Future Crises*. Oxford University Press.

Stark, A. (2019). Policy Learning and the Public Inquiry. *Policy Sciences*, *52*(3), 397–417. https://doi.org/10.1007/s11077-019-09348-0.

Stark, A. (2020). Left on the Shelf: Explaining the Failure of Public Inquiry Recommendations. *Public Administration*, *98*(3), 609–24. https://doi.org/10.1111/padm.12630.

Stark, A. (2023). Measuring Public Inquiry Success. In S. Prasser, (Ed.), *New Directions in Royal Commissions and Public Inquiries: Do We Need Them?* (pp. 195–214). Connorcourt.

Stark, A., & Head, B. (2019). Institutional Amnesia and Public Policy. *Journal of European Public Policy*, *26*(10), 1521–39. https://doi.org/10.1080/13501763.2018.1535612.

Stark, A., & Le, D. (2022). IPPO: Public Inquiry Design Choices: what Ideas Should Be Adopted from Past Inquiries around the World? *IPPO*. 18 January. https://covidandsociety.com/public-inquiry-design-choices-ideas-past-inquiries-around-world/.

Stark, A, Thomson, N. K. and Marston, G. (2021). *Public deliberation and policy design*. Policy Design and Practice, 4(4), 1–13. doi: 10.1080/25741292.2021.1912906.

Stark, A., Punter, H., & Zarrabi, B. (2023). A Return to the Classics? The Implementation of Royal Commissions in Australia. *Australian Journal of Political Science*, *58*(1), 19–36. https://doi.org/10.1080/10361146.2022.2117017.

Stone,D. (2012).*Policy Paradox: The Art of Political Decision Making*. 3rd ed. W. W. Norton & Comp.

Streeck, W., & Thelen, K. (2005). *Beyond Continuity: Institutional Change in Advanced Political Economies*. Oxford University Press.

Sulitzeanu-Kenan, R. (2010). Reflection in the Shadow of Blame: When Do Politicians Appoint Commissions of Inquiry? *British Journal of*

Political Science, 40(3), 613–34. https://doi.org/10.1017/S0007123
410000049.

Thill, C. (2015). Listening for Policy Change: How the Voices of Disabled People Shaped Australia's National Disability Insurance Scheme. *Disability & Society, 30*(1), 15–28. https://doi.org/10.1080/09687599.2014.987220.

Timmins, N. (2019). An Elementary Primer for Politicians and Potential Chairs on Public Inquiries. *The Political Quarterly, 90*(2), 238–44. https://doi.org/10.1111/1467-923X.12699.

Vaughan, D. (2006). NASA Revisited: Theory, Analogy and Public Sociology. *American Journal of Sociology, 112*(2), 353–93.

Vickers, S. G. (1965). *The Art of Judgment: A Study of Policy Making.* Basic Books.

Voß, J.-P., & Simons, A. (2014). Instrument Constituencies and the Supply Side of Policy Innovation: The Social Life of Emissions Trading. *Environmental Politics, 23*(5), 735–54. https://doi.org/10.1080/09644016.2014.923625.

Walsh, J., & Johnson, S. (2013). Development and Principles of the National Disability Insurance Scheme. *Australian Economic Review, 46*(3), 327–37. https://doi.org/10.1111/j.1467-8462.2013.12032.x.

Wellstead, A. M., Gofen, A., & Carter, A. (2021). Policy Innovation Lab Scholarship: Past, Present, and the Future – Introduction to the Special Issue on Policy Innovation Labs. *Policy Design and Practice, 4*(2), 193–211. https://doi.org/10.1080/25741292.2021.1940700.

Yates, S. (2018). *A Critical Frame Analysis of Victoria's Royal Commission into Family Violence.* UNSW. https://doi.org/10.26190/unsworks/21172.

Cambridge Elements ≡

Public Policy

M. Ramesh
National University of Singapore (NUS)

M. Ramesh is UNESCO Chair on Social Policy Design at the Lee Kuan Yew School of Public Policy, NUS. His research focuses on governance and social policy in East and Southeast Asia, in addition to public policy institutions and processes. He has published extensively in reputed international journals. He is Co-editor of *Policy and Society* and *Policy Design and Practice*.

Michael Howlett
Simon Fraser University, British Columbia

Michael Howlett is Burnaby Mountain Professor and Canada Research Chair (Tier 1) in the Department of Political Science, Simon Fraser University. He specialises in public policy analysis, and resource and environmental policy. He is currently editor-in-chief of *Policy Sciences* and co-editor of the *Journal of Comparative Policy Analysis, Policy and Society* and *Policy Design and Practice*.

Xun WU
Hong Kong University of Science and Technology

Xun WU is Professor and Head of the Division of Public Policy at the Hong Kong University of Science and Technology. He is a policy scientist whose research interests include policy innovations, water resource management and health policy reform. He has been involved extensively in consultancy and executive education, his work involving consultations for the World Bank and UNEP.

Judith Clifton
University of Cantabria

Judith Clifton is Professor of Economics at the University of Cantabria, Spain. She has published in leading policy journals and is editor-in-chief of the *Journal of Economic Policy Reform*. Most recently, her research enquires how emerging technologies can transform public administration, a forward-looking cutting-edge project which received €3.5 million funding from the Horizon2020 programme.

Eduardo Araral
National University of Singapore (NUS)

Eduardo Araral is widely published in various journals and books and has presented in forty conferences. He is currently Co-Director of the Institute of Water Policy at the Lee Kuan Yew School of Public Policy, NUS, and is a member of the editorial board of *Journal of Public Administration Research and Theory* and the board of the Public Management Research Association.

About the Series

Elements in Public Policy is a concise and authoritative collection of assessments of the state of the art and future research directions in public policy research, as well as substantive new research on key topics. Edited by leading scholars in the field, the series is an ideal medium for reflecting on and advancing the understanding of critical issues in the public sphere. Collectively, the series provides a forum for broad and diverse coverage of all major topics in the field while integrating different disciplinary and methodological approaches.

Cambridge Elements ≡

Public Policy

Elements in the Series

A full series listing is available at: www.cambridge.org/EPPO

Printed in the United States
by Baker & Taylor Publisher Services